THANKING & BLESSING

—the sacred art

THANKING & BLESSING
—the sacred art

Spiritual Vitality through Gratefulness

JAY MARSHALL, PhD

FOREWORD BY PHILIP GULLEY
AUTHOR OF *ALMOST FRIENDS* AND OTHER *HARMONY* NOVELS

Walking Together, Finding the Way ®
SKYLIGHT PATHS®
PUBLISHING
Woodstock, Vermont

Thanking & Blessing—The Sacred Art:
Spiritual Vitality through Gratefulness

For information regarding permission to reprint material from this book, please mail or fax your request in writing to SkyLight Paths Publishing, Permissions Department, at the address / fax number listed below, or e-mail your request to permissions@skylightpaths.com.

Library of Congress Cataloging-in-Publication Data
Marshall, Jay W. (Jay Wade), 1959–
    Thanking and blessing—the sacred art : spiritual vitality through gratefulness / by Jay Marshall.
        p. cm.
    Includes bibliographical references.
    ISBN-13: 978-1-59473-231-7
    ISBN-10: 1-59473-231-0
    1. Gratitude—Religious aspects. 2. Spirituality. 3. Conduct of life. I. Title.

BL65.G73M37 2007
204'.4—dc22
                                                                    2007029267

10 9 8 7 6 5 4 3 2 1

SkyLight Paths Publishing is creating a place where people of different spiritual traditions come together for challenge and inspiration, a place where we can help each other understand the mystery that lies at the heart of our existence.

SkyLight Paths sees both believers and seekers as a community that increasingly transcends traditional boundaries of religion and denomination—people wanting to learn from each other, *walking together, finding the way.*

Manufactured in the United States of America
Cover Design: Jenny Buono
SkyLight Paths, "Walking Together, Finding the Way" and colophon are trademarks of LongHill Partners, Inc., registered in the U.S. Patent and Trademark Office.

Walking Together, Finding the Way®
Published by SkyLight Paths Publishing
A Division of LongHill Partners, Inc.
Sunset Farm Offices, Route 4, P.O. Box 237
Woodstock, VT 05091
Tel: (802) 457-4000   Fax: (802) 457-4004
www.skylightpaths.com

To my wife, Judi,
who each day is an example of the wonder
of God's blessings!

CONTENTS

FOREWORD

by Philip Gulley

I heard about Jay Marshall before I met him. Rumors had been circulating in the Quaker world of a bright young man pastoring a meeting on the other side of the state. The Quaker cosmos is a small one—there are more Baptists in Birmingham than there are Quakers in the world—so our paths eventually crossed at one of the myriad conferences Quakers hold to save the world and whales and whatever else has captured our imaginations.

Like Jay, I am a Quaker pastor with a day job. Jay is dean of the Earlham School of Religion in Richmond, Indiana. I write books about God and God's people and lots of other things. But our first love is ministry, that curious vocation that is simultaneously joyful and exasperating. Those of us in it speak in hallowed tones about God calling us to it. But sometimes ministry feels like the punch line of a divine joke. These days, pastoral tenure is shorter than the shelf life of bread. But Jay has persisted in ministry with humor, optimism, and good cheer, for twenty-five years. This wonderful book, *Thanking and Blessing—The Sacred Art: Spiritual Vitality through Gratefulness*, reveals something of the outlook that has informed his work. Indeed, has often made his work seem more like play.

Thanksgiving and blessing are deceptive topics, innocent on the face of it, but potentially dangerous concepts when one starts tinkering with them. In one of the Apostle Paul's earliest letters, he implored the saints in Thessalonica to "rejoice always, pray without ceasing, and give thanks in all circumstances" (1 Thess. 5:16–18a). It is these kind of sweeping generalizations that drive us theologicaltypes mad and keep us up nights.

Give thanks in all circumstances? Hmmm…. Off the top of my head I can think of a dozen events in the past year that don't elicit my gratitude—two children killed at a railroad crossing, a close friend's diagnosis of leukemia, another friend's painful death from cancer, a neighbor's bitter divorce, another friend's bankruptcy and loss of home, the sudden death of a friend's child from a devastating virus.

In the last example, I went to sit with the mother and father. I didn't know what to say except that I was sorry. When parents lose a child, people often react by never mentioning the child's name again, believing it will spare the parents further pain. But parents like to think their child mattered, that people remember their child and think well of him or her. So I talked about what their daughter had meant to me, how I had enjoyed our regular conversations at the candy store where she worked in our small town.

They began to weep. "We've heard from so many friends," the mother said. "We feel so blessed to be so cared for."

Blessed?

I'm beginning to wonder if thanksgiving and blessing aren't human impulses, hard-wired in our humanity, always underneath the surface and waiting for the slightest reason to bubble up and over.

I've lately been drawn to three writers who expound the virtues of atheism—Sam Harris, Richard Dawkins, and Christopher Hitchens. They make much sense, distressingly so for a man who's spent his life believing otherwise. But none of the three have adequately answered a nagging question of mine—Who do I thank for my children? Who do I thank in the evening when I'm walking with my wife and the western sky is streaked with pink and the breeze is soft in my face and life is so incomparably good?

This is why I return to thanksgiving, why our instinct toward gratitude seems so natural, even in the darkest of days, and why I am so profoundly grateful to Jay Marshall for adding flesh to the bones of blessing, clearing the dim from life's mirror, so we might see ourselves and God a little better.

INTRODUCTION

Over the years, I have become convinced of at least one fundamental truth: God wants to be in relationship with us. Just how each of us goes about establishing and maintaining that relationship in ways that we find meaningful and fulfilling becomes what we might call our own unique forms of spirituality.

No one method of spirituality will work for everybody, but in my decades of personal spiritual exploration and professional ministerial experience, I have discovered a powerful pair of concepts that, when observed and practiced intentionally, can keep your relationship with God dynamic and alive: thanking, on the one hand; and blessing, on the other.

These two concepts are similar but not identical. Thanking is an act by which I express thankfulness to God (or another person) for some specific benefit or favor. It is a response in kind. It is rooted in gratitude for that specific benefit or favor, and as such is focused in its scope. Nevertheless, thanking, when practiced, can change—and has changed—the way I see the world.

Blessing, on the other hand, is an act by which I *initiate* bringing goodness, holiness, or something of God's presence into the world around me. The act of blessing is also rooted in gratitude, but not in response to a particular gift or benefit. Rather, it arises from a profound awareness of God's deep, abiding, and lasting presence with me and in our world. Blessing is not a response in kind, but rather a way of finding unique and creative ways of manifesting God's invisible presence in the world about me—often with prayers and well wishes called, appropriately enough, "blessings." Yet, blessing can take many forms.

Taken together and intentionally cultivated as a spiritual practice, thanking and blessing are raised to the level of a spiritual art—a particular lifestyle, a way of viewing and interacting with the world that nurtures a healthy relationship with God, with other people, and even with yourself. Practicing thanking and blessing helps you remember that the world is a place of abundance, and more than that, practicing the sacred art of thanking and blessing lets you actively contribute to that abundance.

WHAT'S IN A NAME?

The fundamental gratitude that gives rise to both thanking and blessing doesn't simply come from nowhere. It comes from the foundational ways that you understand and picture God, what you were taught God was like, even the very names you learned to use when talking about God.

I was fortunate enough to be steeped in an atmosphere of church, faith, and God from my earliest childhood, and it suited my inquisitive personality well. While I joined other boys in playing typical kid games such as cowboys and Indians, when no one was around I sometimes amused myself by pretending that I was a preacher. When I was eleven or twelve years old, a Sunday school teacher dismissed me from class because I told her the questions she asked were too easy. To this day, my aunts enjoy reminding me of the Sunday when, as a preschooler, I interrupted the pastor's sermon and asked him to repeat himself because I did not understand what he meant. Although some people tried to teach me that God was in the business of delivering holy monologues in the form of dogma, creeds, and commandments to be blindly obeyed, I didn't believe them. Even back then, God for me was something to be experienced. I thought God wanted to have a conversation, a relationship.

I was fortunate that my own Quaker tradition has a deep respect for personal experience. This is a boon for inquisitive people like me who prefer to discover for ourselves rather than accept what is handed down to us. This has been one of Quakerism's great gifts to me—affirming my own experience that God is indeed a God who wants to have a conversation, a relationship, with me. Unlike other traditions that conceive of God as distant, hostile, or disinterested, Quakers' emphasis on Jesus' statement in John 15, "I have called you friends," portrays a God who is approachable, understanding, and wanting to help—qualities that engender gratitude in me.

Indeed, the names we use for God have deep implications. Quakers conceive of God as Friend, but Quaker circles are also fond of the metaphor of light and, in particular, the phrase "Inner Light." This understanding of God also has its origin in the Gospel of John,[1] where the term emphasizes God's searching and illuminating activity. God searches and knows our hearts—our thoughts and our attitudes. God's light shines on our inner musings, helping us to clearly see things—including our own motivations—as God sees them. This Inner Light serves as a guide, inviting us to consider matters carefully. Quakers love to wait, ponder, and contemplate as we consider what it is we can learn or could do in response to the Light. Things appear differently when viewed with the help of the divine Inner Light.

God as Friend and God as Inner Light—I share these two metaphors at the outset for two reasons. First, it defines my relationship with God as Friend, as Inner Light, as an honest, trustworthy presence. The universe may be vast, but I feel connected with its source of power and life because I am in conversation with the Divine. Life may be chaotic, but I am not alone. My response to this One who befriends me, converses with me, and accompanies me is gratitude—the foundation for both thanking and blessing.

The second reason for sharing the metaphors is to invite you to begin trying the art of thanking and blessing by thinking about the names and metaphors you use for God. What do they tell you about your understanding of God's identity and involvement in your life? How do they shape your current spiritual practices? Do they invite a feeling of intimacy with God? Or do they foster a sense of alienation? What would happen if you began to think of God differently? Are they conducive to gratitude, or do they engender fear, guilt, or some other emotion?

It seems those early days of pretending to be a preacher had a lasting effect on me. It has now been twenty-five years since I first entered a college classroom as a student because I felt God calling me to serve as a minister. Nearly a decade in higher education, fifteen years as a pastoral minister, many years as dean of a Quaker seminary, and several stints in the classroom as a teacher have brought many answers, as well as introduced new questions. I treasure each of those experiences, but more important to me than the experiences themselves is the ongoing conversation with the Divine I have enjoyed. In my opinion, our most authentic and dynamic spiritual moments are rooted in our ongoing conversation with the Divine. What we call faith is our effort to live in ways that demonstrate the effects of those conversations with God, because they allow us to continually discover new ways of relating to God, new names by which we can describe the Divine, and the gratitude that can give rise to this life-changing sacred art of thanking and blessing.

Let's now explore the sacred art of thanking and blessing in more detail.

THANKING EXPRESSES GRATITUDE

The act of thanking another person for something he or she has done for us is an act of common decency and a sign of good manners. When we thank someone, whether through a verbal thank-you, an acknowledging smile or hug, a written note, or even a good deed, we express our gratitude or appreciation.

In everyday contexts, we have many opportunities to thank others. When someone shares her umbrella in the rain, I thank her for offering protection from the weather. If a friend invites me to dinner, I thank him because I value the hospitality and fellowship he offers. But the act of thanking is, or should be, more than a mechanical response born out of obligation. Whatever form it takes, it is an expression of the gratitude, you might even say praise, we feel in response to the way someone else has enriched our lives. The act of thanking allows us to experience the graciousness of the other's act more deeply.

But how might we thank God? When it comes to thanking in a spiritual or religious context, our thanksgiving often takes some form of prayer or worship, although we are by no means limited to these expressions. The psalmist in the Hebrew Bible demonstrates that thanking is a response to God's activity on humanity's behalf. "Let them thank the Lord for his steadfast love, for his wonderful works to humankind" (Ps. 107:8, NRSV) or "I will thank you forever, because of what you have done" (Ps. 52:9, NRSV). When the apostle Paul instructs Christians on how to live their lives, he includes "giving thanks to God the Father at all times and for everything in the name of our Lord Jesus Christ" (Eph. 5:20). Thanking is a regular part of my conversation with God. I give thanks for life, for family, for blues skies, and for rainy days. I offer thanks for the intimacy that comes with experiencing God as friend. I even thank God for moments that challenge me and cause me to struggle, because I learn new things from them. I see all these things as gifts from God, and by offering thanks I acknowledge them as such.

But whatever the context, the act of thanking helps us acknowledge both the presence of the giver and our gratitude for the gift. It reiterates in our consciousness that we are not alone; that we are connected directly to God and to others; that despite what we may feel at other times, in fact, we have much to be thankful for. What response does God elicit from you? Can you remember moments of sincere thanking? What would it take for you to be able to thank God on a regular basis?

BLESSING INFUSES HOLY GOODNESS

If thanking is a response to an act of kindness, then blessing is our way of initiating an act of kindness. That said, thanking and blessing do have much in common. The most notable overlap just might be what occurs before eating: we bless the food by saying a "blessing" because we are grateful for the abundance of the earth that produced the food, the abundance of our finances to secure it, and the abundance of time to prepare it. At the same time, we are grateful for this particular meal itself, stretched before us on the table. Hence, it's no surprise that this pre-meal ritual is also often called "giving thanks."

As with thanking, the act of blessing can be directed toward God via "blessings" such as hymns and prayers, or toward fellow human beings as kind words. Yet our experience of blessing is different; in some sense, we are on the other side of the equation (we might even receive thanks for our blessing). The ground of gratitude that gives rise to our impulse to bless is much wider, much deeper, than for that of thanking. We are aware not of a particular act or moment in time; rather, we are slowly and continually aware of God's constant presence in our experience, of the great flow of gifts in our lives. We draw on this reality in order to bless a situation, whether by infusing goodness or humor into a bleak moment, by wishing well to those embarking on a lengthy journey or task, or even by making a solemn promise of aid or faithfulness.

Several years ago, I knew a man who made a commitment to visit the residents of a local nursing home for an hour or so every Sunday morning. He had no family members in the facility. He had no longtime friends there to whom he felt obliged. He was a car salesman, not a chaplain. But he knew that many of these individuals had few, if any, visitors, and little to look forward to other than a day staring at the ceiling or sitting in a wheelchair parked in the hallway. So each Sunday he went to offer a smile, a warm touch, a brief conversation. Each time he did, he brought joy to the place, lifted their spirits, and infused a bit of goodness into their day. This was blessing in action.

Blessing is a word saturated with religious nuance, and for good reason. As noted above, blessing is an action associated with divine activity toward creation and humanity. Some traditional prayers include phrases and rituals of blessing so that offering blessings to God is part of the religious practice. Other traditions have rituals of blessing that consecrate places or occasions. As religious blessing infuses goodness, it also elevates our awareness of the Divine, so that life is spiced with holiness.

But blessing doesn't have to take a ritualized form. Quakers are low on liturgy—you might think of us as liturgically challenged! But we are dedicated to integrating spiritual practice with everyday events, even the seemingly mundane ones. The act of blessing can be as simple as when you share an encouraging word with someone else and thereby inspire optimism in an otherwise bleak day. A blessing could come in the form of a gift you give—any type, in fact—that raises the recipient's spirits and expectations about his or her future potential and possibilities. A blessing infuses goodness into the moment, with effects that linger far beyond its initial delivery.

For example, certain relationships—with friends or mentors, for instance—bless me. A friend of mine has an incredible ability to improve my state of mind with something as simple as a telephone call. He is a Quaker in North Carolina, and he contacts me every few weeks. Sometimes he wants information. Other times he has an idea that might be useful to consider at the school where I am dean. Or he may just call to see how I am. But whatever the reason, he invariably lifts my spirits. Why? Because he takes an interest in my life. He supports my ideas, even when he points out possible weaknesses in them. He has an active mind and reads widely, so he always has something new and interesting to share. He values and supports *me* as a person. People like my friend create an optimistic, encouraging setting in which I view the world and think about my participation in it. They influence my state of mind and my outlook on life. I, myself, begin to act in ways that share goodness and hope with others.

HOW TO USE THIS BOOK

The twin themes of thanking and blessing, when practiced together intentionally, form a unique approach to spirituality that can enrich your life and transform your relationship with God, with others, even with yourself.

If you are a seeker of truth and meaning, you might find practicing the sacred art of thanking and blessing helpful if:

- You want a spirituality that cultivates a sense of intimacy with the Divine.
- You are ready for a spirituality that emphasizes blessing rather than fear, love rather than condemnation.
- You are interested in thinking about faith in ways that emphasize the unity we have with all creation.
- You think that every one of us has value in the eyes of God.
- You are searching for an inclusive faith eager to undertake reconciliation in a greatly divided world.
- You refuse to settle for religious practices that do not engage the world's most pressing issues, such as prejudice, hatred, poverty, and inequality.

The principles of thanking and blessing are universal. Though I present them here from a Christian, specifically Quaker, perspective, they can be easily adapted and practiced by people of any and all faiths. The art of thanking and blessing offers a uniquely powerful way to keep ourselves rooted in gratitude, even in trying situations. Thanking and blessing infuse goodness in relationships of all kinds—personal, professional, divine—so that stability, health, and wholeness are achievable. And, thanking and blessing make life worth living!

This introduction to the sacred art of thanking and blessing aims not so much to define what thanking and blessing are, but rather to give you the tools to recognize them and cultivate them in your life and in the life of those around you. I will encourage you to contemplate how you think about God and how you tell your own spiritual story. Neither is set in stone, and you have the option to revise them. I will ask you to sit in silence—not for the sake of doing nothing, but in order to practice waiting for God in holy expectation. I will supply you with ways to begin conversations with the Divine, to get acquainted if you are not already old friends. I will nudge you to wrestle with the implications of that kinship, and to inspect your attitudes and assumptions toward those around you. I want you to remember that this world is God's world, and encourage you to expect to meet your Friend throughout the day in places that might surprise you. As you recognize the Divine around you, you will experience the world as a more welcoming place because it is no longer foreign territory, even when you don't know where you are. I will suggest ways for you to bless the people around you—those you love and even those you would rather avoid. By the end of our journey together, I hope you will embody a commitment to live in dialogue with the Holy and to understand what it means to live a life of thanking and blessing—as an expression of your own joy and as your contribution to God's continuing creative work around us.

In the following pages, I will more fully explore the concepts of thanking and blessing as they relate to our religious, spiritual, personal, and professional lives. It begins with understanding that our spiritual stories begin with God's original blessing (not cursing), which sets the positive, optimistic trajectory for everything that follows. We will explore the practice of expectant waiting, which allows us to encounter God deep within ourselves and makes us aware of our Inner Witness—that gentle (and sometimes not so gentle) nudging that guides us to make wise and holy choices. As we discover more of God in our daily affairs, we can learn to live sacramentally, where every moment and every encounter holds the potential to be a holy one. This, in turn, allows us to (in the words of Quaker George Fox) "walk cheerfully over the earth," engaging with life actively with a positive disposition, which in turn is reflected back to us. Fox also reminds us that we are called to "answer that of God" in other people; this, too, is part of the sacred art of thanking and blessing: acknowledging that every person is made in the image of God and responding accordingly. We will also explore the role of thanking and blessing in creation itself, in practicing hospitality, in the power of hope to motivate and guide us, in the power of integrity to ground our lives, in the role our practice of thanking and blessing can have in transforming the lives of others, and in how it contributes to solving the problems that plague our world. Lest this remain theoretical, every chapter concludes with practical steps you can take to deepen your practice of thanking and blessing. Finally, it is worth noting that when I include quotations from the Hebrew Bible, I follow the English translation of the Jewish Publication Society's 1985 Tanakh, unless otherwise noted. New Testament citations follow the New Revised Standard Version translation.

MY HOPES FOR YOU

About halfway through my fifteen years in pastoral ministry, I realized it was not my responsibility to dictate what others thought or believed. My best gift was merely to help introduce them to the Divine—to help them stumble into an "Aha!" moment where they were grasped by God and simultaneously had some grasp of God. Once the introduction was made, the rest was really up to the person and God.

The journey described here has a similar intent—it gently invites you toward an "Aha!" moment where you are fundamentally and wholly loved by God, blessed, at home in the world and comfortable with yourself. Such a realization is transformational both to you and to those around you. They will notice the difference as you become eager to make a positive difference in this life and world. Truly, a little thanking and blessing go a long way!

CHAPTER ONE

BLESSED BEGINNINGS

The beginning of any story is its most crucial part, for in those first few words or phrases or paragraphs the trajectory is set for the rest of the tale. The very way we go about interpreting and understanding the rest of the story is bound up with the tenor of that opening. When we hear the words "Once upon a time," for example, we immediately assume that whatever comes next is part of a fairy tale. No matter how factual or real-life the details of the story become, our minds will continually refer back to that beginning—"Once upon a time"—and make judgments about the material accordingly. The beginning of a story has remarkable power.

This is certainly true of stories we read in literature. But this is also true of our personal life and faith stories, for they too had a beginning, one that lay down for us certain core assumptions, beliefs, and attitudes that we continually refer to—consciously or not—to help us interpret the details of our lives. As with the beginning of a fairy tale, the beginnings of our personal and faith stories have remarkable power.

My own story is a good example of this. I grew up as part of a hardworking, farming family in the rural South, where I experienced a variety of powerful voices that were intent on marginalizing me and labeling me unworthy. Schoolmates conveyed their parents' prejudices that folks from the country were not as socially acceptable as those who lived in town. A high school guidance counselor insulted my entire family the day she refused my registration in an agriculture class because I was "too smart to be a farmer." Even the national media perpetuated insulting stereotypes about Southern accents, the presumed lower intelligence of people born in the South, and worse—as portrayed in the movie *Deliverance*, for example. Those powerful messages, though untrue, were hard to ignore. They took their toll, breaking the spirits of some and inciting rage in others.

Yet the beginning of my life story was not one of defeat, but rather one of strong love and empowerment. The nourishment that allowed me to flourish came largely from my parents, and especially my mother, who continually demonstrated her love for me. Photographs and home movies show that love in action—my mother's warm embrace or my father blowing out a three-year-old's birthday candles because I had bad aim. Their love established a stable, positive base from which it was easy to explore and learn. They supported my interests—from playing Little League baseball, to learning piano, to biking around the community to sell personalized Christmas cards door to door. From this beginning I grew up believing I could accomplish anything I set my mind to, and this gave me a lasting sense of empowerment that shaped my worldview into adulthood.

Our spiritual stories deserve the same type of positive beginning. Many Christians, including those of my own Quaker tradition, choose to trace the origins of their faith to Genesis chapters 2 and 3, which recount the story of Adam and Eve's expulsion from the Garden of Eden, or what is popularly known as The Fall. For these people, the story of their faith and spirituality begins with *failure*. With that kind of beginning to the story, it's no great mystery when even those whose faith is strong find themselves struggling to find a powerful and richly rewarding spirituality that affirms and celebrates life.

But our spiritual stories (from whatever tradition) don't have to start with failure. I prefer to let my story begin at the beginning, with Genesis 1. There we find not shame, fear, and failure, but rather exuberance, delight, and the celebration of creation.

> And God said, "Let the waters teem with living creatures and birds fly above the earth."… So God created the great creatures of the sea … and every winged bird according to its kind … and God saw that it was good. God blessed them and said, "Be fruitful and increase in number." (Gen. 1:20–22)

The beginning of this story is one of blessing—when God blesses all of creation. It is a beginning to a spiritual story that encourages and empowers.

The story of original blessing isn't unique to faith traditions that trace their origins to the Book of Genesis. Other religions and spiritual paths have creation stories rooted in original blessing.

> He (the Divine Self), desiring to produce beings of many kinds from his own body, first with a thought created the waters, and placed his seed in them. That seed became a golden egg, in brilliancy equal to the sun." (Hinduism, Laws of Manu)[1]

> We created man of an extraction of clay, then We set him, a drop, in a receptacle secure … thereafter We produced him as another creature. So blessed be God, the fairest of creators! (Islam, Qur'an 23:14)

So He thought He would create an earth; therefore He took from His body a piece of earth and rolled it into a ball in the palms of His hands, and then He threw it below Him, and it became the earth.... The four spiritual beings that were placed in the four directions of the earth were empowered to govern the winds and they were also empowered to bless mankind their particular kind of power or strength. Then He created all things and placed the humans here on earth in the midst of them. (Native American [Winnebago], The Medicine Rite Foundation Myth)[2]

While the details of these stories differ, each story tells us that God created us, as part of the creation, in order to be in relationship with us. Creation—both the act of, and the results of—is God's blessing. As part of God's creation, we are then, in turn, inherently part of, and recipients of, God's blessing. This is where the sacred art of thanking and blessing begins.

PART OF GOD'S BLESSING, BLESSED BY GOD

In Genesis 1, God creates with word and deed. A formless void becomes a vibrant world, complete with light and darkness, dry land and seas, vegetation and animal life—and human beings. In the beginning, there was only the act of creation and the pronouncement not just that creation was "good" but also that, in being blessed, all of creation was *favored by* God.

While Genesis states that "God blessed them," on a more fundamental level, God's blessing of creation was inherent in the act of creation itself, for by creating the heavens and the earth and everything in them, including us, God established a bond, a relationship, between God and creation.

We can understand this same principle in the profound bond between parent and child. Children are a part of us and makes us who we are. It's hard to explain just how deeply parents want their kids to be happy, successful, comfortable, and safe. These are blessings that parents want for their children as deeply, if not more so, as if they were wishing them for themselves, and most parents will do everything in their power to bless them as much as they can.

When we turn to the sacred scriptures of the world's great religions, we see that God plays the same role as the parent for us:

> You are children of the Lord your God.
> (Deut. 14:1)

> I am Father and Mother of the world. (Bhagavad Gita 9.17)

> All [human] creatures are God's children, and those dearest to God are the ones who treat His children kindly. (Hadith of Baihaqi)

> See what love the Father has given us, that we should be called children of God; and that is what we are. (1 John 3:1)

Just as parents want the blessings of abundance, comfort, happiness, and safety for their children, so too God wants these blessings for us as part of creation.

MANIFESTING GOD'S BLESSING

One of the remarkable things about God's original blessing is that it continues to this day. You can tap into it at any time and, indeed, be an instrument of that blessing for others.

But how?

There are at least three things you can do to engage and perpetuate God's blessing that occurs all around you. These three things are:

1. Embrace the idea that God created us all in the divine image.
2. Recognize the proof of God's favor.
3. Acknowledge that everyone around you was also created in God's image, and interact with them accordingly, in a Godlike way.

BLESS AS GOD BLESSES

The creation account in Genesis 1 describes it this way:

> God created man in the image of himself, in the image of God he created him, male and female he created them. God blessed them, saying to them, "Be fruitful, multiply, fill the earth" and God saw everything that he had made, and indeed, it was very good. (Gen. 1:31)

The claim that God created men and women "in the image of God" has been fodder for theological debates for millennia, and no consensus has emerged on what this ultimately means. Yet with regard to our topic, God didn't simply bless us as part of creation; God created us in such a way that we can emulate the activity of God. In Leviticus 19:2, God asks us to "Be Holy as I, God, am Holy." We can take this to mean that if God creates, then we can create. If God blesses, then we can bless. God created us in a way that we are able to bring positive, creative energy to life's activities. As we do, we become participants in God's creative work.

One of my favorite ways to participate in God's creative work is by having probing conversations with others. Several people have observed that I have a natural tendency to ask questions that provoke introspection and healthy change. During a recent conversation, I asked a friend how many days per year she traveled offering workshops and volunteering her time. I asked out of genuine interest, and I made no comment or value judgment of her answer, although I was genuinely amazed at her pace. Some weeks later, she e-mailed to explain that she was reducing her travel and volunteer work because my question prompted her to examine the pace of her life. I have had countless conversations with others that began with them saying, "Remember when you asked me … ?" I believe that asking honest questions in conversations introduces creative energy, and more important, personal reflection, so that blessing in the form of positive, personal change can occur. This is one way I participate in God's creative work, although there are many others, such as caring for others, animals, and the environment; volunteering time or donating to worthy causes; and learning to truly listen to others.

Remembering that we are made in the image of God is one part of embracing the blessing of our creation, but there is a bit more to our story than that. It is also a matter of understanding God's continuing, intimate connection with us. The Hindu tradition describes the human heart as one of God's dwelling places: "Truly do I exist in all beings, but I am most manifest in man. The human heart is my favorite dwelling place" (Srimad Bhagavatam 11.2). Similarly, the Talmud talks of God dwelling within humanity: "Let a man always consider himself as if the Holy One dwells within him" (Talmud, *Taanit* 11b). In the Christian New Testament, Jesus spoke of a Divine-human relationship in which one dwells within the other: "Abide in me as I abide in you. Just as the branch cannot bear fruit by itself unless it abides in the vine, neither can you unless you abide in me" (John 15:4).

These traditions possess an amazing consistency on this point. God chooses to dwell within us. So not only are we made in the divine image, but God remains intimately close to us as well.

BLESSED BY DIVINE FAVOR

The second step in engaging God's blessing is to recognize the proof of God's favor. Each of us is absolutely swimming in a sea of divine blessings! We need only to pause and look carefully at the world around us. Go out for a walk in the forest and pay attention to the towering trees. Look up at the sky and let its vast expanse speak to you. Take a slow drive through arid deserts and hear the silent praise offered by its stark beauty. Hike into deep canyons where every sound echoes as its contribution to the choir. There is so much to behold, and even more to discover and experience.

I need only to step into my vegetable garden to come face to face with a smorgasbord of divine blessing. Each April as I till the soil and prepare the rows, God reminds me of the mystery of life. I stuff seeds into the darkness, where they break open, and tender sprouts force their way to the surface. Every year, I marvel when the seedlings appear and wonder that it happens at all. Like an overprotective parent, I defend them against predators—weeds that would choke them, insects that would devour them—and I learn again the blessing of God's provision as plants mature and tomato blossoms turn into tender fruits and sweet potatoes push themselves up near the soil's surface. As harvest time arrives, I stand amazed at what has grown from those tiny seeds, and feel blessed to realize that I have been a participant in this nourishing process.

In such moments we begin to experience the reality of divine love more than merely understanding it. Blessing becomes more than a warm, fuzzy idea; it is a way of viewing the beauty and complexity of the world around us, noticing how the countless parts create an incredible whole. The universe starts to feel more comfortable, friendly, and soothing. We are neither out of place nor out of the ordinary. We belong, and can proudly be counted as part of the good and blessed created order.

SHARING BLESSINGS

Once we acknowledge that we are recipients of original blessing, and recognize proof of God's favor in the world around us, the third step is to live accordingly. That is to say, just as we are created in the divine image, so too is everyone around us. When we engage others as Godlike, our interactions become inherently holy.

Go to a busy mall or an outdoor café, find a comfortable seat, and watch people—our assorted shapes, sizes, colors, and cultures. Despite our differences, we share the most common and important of features: we all are part of this incredible creation that was blessed and described as good. Collectively, we are a manifestation of divine blessing. Once we acknowledge this, we experience a transformation of perspective and worldview. Our role is much simpler—to manifest the reality of blessing— one that views the world positively, marvels at the encounters with the Divine that are available in every moment, and celebrates the possibilities before us and within us. In the words of the great twentieth-century Jewish theologian Abraham Joshua Heschel, "Just to be is a blessing. Just to live is holy."[3]

Pause for a moment and consider the beginning of your own faith story. Where does it begin? How does it begin? With failure? With blessing? With something else? Where does God appear in it? How do you understand the relationship of the Divine with the world? With yourself?

How would you describe your understanding of God? Can you easily imagine God's love for you being special? What does the idea that you are created in the image of God suggest to you about yourself?

EXPERIMENTING WITH BLESSING

We begin the journey down the sacred path of thanking and blessing with small, simple steps. The following are some useful methods that I have discovered for encouraging an outlook that will help you experience God's original blessing for yourself and give you tools to share that blessing with others in a sacred way.

As you read through these practices and find that some appeal to you, remember that it's important to be gentle with yourself. The idea is to discover original blessing with joy, not to enforce some new agenda on yourself!

WORKING WITH SACRED TEXTS

One place to begin discovering a sense of original blessing is with a sacred text of your choice. Sacred texts offer you the wisdom of previous generations who sought to know and understand the Divine. These texts are often presented as authorities to be accepted at face value, but their real value lies in their ability to assist our efforts to encounter the Divine in a living, powerful way. Particularly useful are sacred texts that elevate the theme of divine blessing and love for creation, and especially for humanity. Psalm 8 and Psalm 104 of the Hebrew Bible are two of my favorites.

Here is a suggested method for exploring the sacred text of your choice:

- Choose a passage from the Bible or other sacred text that is meaningful to you. Begin with a short text, something that you can read in a few minutes.
- Spend a certain amount of time each morning reading and rereading the passage. Reading it multiple times helps you to penetrate the first layer and see meanings lying beneath the surface. Try reading it quickly, slowly, out loud. Each method will tend to reveal something new to you.
- Allow yourself to pause over any images or phrases that you find compelling or significant. Why do you find them so?
- Use a journal to record your experiences. If you have any questions, write those down, too. Dwell on the questions, ask about them in prayer, or seek out someone who can provide you with a perspective on possible answers.
- In time, perhaps days, weeks, or longer, you are likely to begin to experience a blessing in the form of encountering

the spirit behind the text. You will learn that a sacred text is more than the words on the page. It is the meaning God gives it as you ponder its nuances and possibilities.

Because of my background, texts associated with the Christian tradition are my first choice, but I learn from the sacred writings of other traditions as well. As I encounter familiar themes, I begin to see bridges of connection. Those bridges welcome me to come as a guest and listen to other versions of the story, to share in the insights of others, and to draw me into a deeper conversation with the Divine.

FINDING BLESSINGS IN SACRED SPACE

Encounters with God are not limited to texts. Many traditions teach that God can be encountered throughout creation. Nevertheless, some places remind us of God's blessing more easily than others. These places can feel like holy ground or sacred space. A useful way to cultivate this awareness of blessing is to spend time in a favorite place and to do so with a conscious awareness that God's blessing is present and surrounding you there.

Here are some strategies for finding and enjoying your sacred space:

- Identify the places where you most easily sense the presence of the Holy. How do you recognize the Holy around you? It may be when you are surprised by joy or soothed by an inner peace. It could be when you feel the distinct presence of the Other, or where a sense of reverence tingles your spine. Know yourself well enough to recognize when you are being greeted by the Divine—and know which places help that happen for you!

- Make space in your schedule to spend time in at least one of your favorite places. Do this on a regular basis, because the goal is to cultivate a more consistent awareness of God.
- Think about what makes those places sacred space for you. Is it the location? Is it the scenery? Is it the quiet solitude, or the presence of other people? How do they help you see the divine blessing that surrounds you?
- Be observant. Notice what is around you—colors, shapes, light, life forms. If your place is outdoors, notice the terrain. Smell the aroma of the soil. Know that whether by nourishing plants or by providing a foundation for a building, it contributes to the blessing of life. With each waving tree branch you see or singing bird you hear, rejoice in its place in creation. If your sacred space is indoors, consider the architecture and the décor. Consider how they set the mood for the space. Wherever your spaces are, be aware that this is holy ground for you.
- If it seems valuable, develop a simple ritual for use in these places, such as offering brief prayers of thanksgiving, taking a walk, sketching a picture, or singing a song. Whatever you do, do it with an awareness that God accompanies you.
- Pay attention to how you feel after spending time in these sacred places. Expect refreshment and a sense of renewal.

For me, knowing my sacred space is important. The woods surrounding my home are holy ground for me. So is my vegetable garden, where soil, sweat, silence, and the sun provide the context for a religious moment. They help me to be mindful of God, creation, and life's abundant blessings.

IN THE HERE, IN THE NOW

The next step is to practice being fully present wherever you are and with whomever you find yourself, for we are all made in the image of God. Being attentive is your contribution to the possibilities of blessing that may emerge in any encounter.

This isn't always easy. On days when I have a demanding schedule, my mind often wants to prepare for what is coming next rather than to listen intently to the person standing before me. In moments when it seems I cannot listen for one more second to the person droning on about something that doesn't catch my interest, my eyes glaze over while I escape to a more interesting place. The problem with this, besides being rude, is that I may miss the blessing that these moments hold for both me and the other person.

Here are a few suggestions for living in the here and now:

- Temporarily stop multitasking! You can resume the practice later, if necessary. Multitasking divides your attention, which can distract your concentration on the matter immediately before you.

- For each task that makes its way onto your "to do" list, undertake it as though your work is a gift to God and to the world. Try to imagine its place in the larger flow of life. If it is filling the car with gasoline, consider the blessing of mobility and transportation. If it is attending a board meeting, remember that your actions and inactions affect people served by decisions the board makes.

- Remember that each person who stands before you is created in the image of God, just as you are. Name for yourself a few ways this person reminds you of God's presence and blessing.

- Practice listening intently to what others say to you. Give them your full attention. Even if their topic is of no interest to you, try to learn why it matters to them. What can you learn from this encounter? What can you offer to the person before you?

Living in the here and now simply means that your awareness of God—who dwells within you and others—invites you to be continually attentive to the blessings that are all around you right now.

NAME YOUR BLESSINGS

Familiarity numbs our senses and may prevent us from seeing the ways that our lives are blessed. This is particularly true if we succumb to our culture's ubiquitous advertising slogans that tell us happiness can only be found in accumulating more and more material goods. While most of us know that such an attitude is madness, it's not always easy to escape the belief that the grass is greener on the other side of the fence.

If you want to raise your awareness of how blessed you are already, try this simple exercise.

1. Find a quiet place. With pad and pencil beside you, spend some time thinking about those persons, events, or attitudes that bring joy to your life. Write those on your pad.
2. Review each name or item on your list. What are the ways each one enriches your life? What would you lack if the person or item were suddenly absent from your life? Note these things on your pad as well. You have just named some of the most significant blessings in your life.

In the course of life's normal routines, you can lose sight of how blessed you are. Exercises like this one provide a reality check. God is near. Life is rich. You are blessed.

Cultivating your awareness of divine blessing will enrich your life. But it will also liberate you to be an agent of blessing. Where you start your story sets the trajectory for what will follow. Let the story of your spiritual journey begin with blessing.

EXPECTANT WAITING

I detest standing in lines. To me, waiting on queue feels like a monumental waste of time. And though I do my best to avoid it, no matter where I go—supermarkets, department stores, lunch buffets—I seem doomed to always choose the slowest line. I think this might be the universe's way of having a laugh at my expense. After all, in the grand scheme of life, lingering a few extra minutes to get through airport security or pay for groceries might be a minor inconvenience. On the other hand, five minutes here, five minutes there, adds up. It is, in fact, time and productivity wasted. It is lost time.

Or is it? Given my impatience with waiting around, the fact that my chosen spiritual discipline identifies waiting—specifically what it calls *expectant waiting*—as a central spiritual practice is an irony that is not lost on me. Expectant waiting is just that, waiting in stillness in anticipation of an encounter with the Divine. It is the next step in the practice of the sacred art of thanking and blessing.

But just how does expectant waiting work? In Quaker tradition, expectant waiting is a somewhat formalized practice that plays a central role in worship. It can, however, be practiced anywhere, anytime—such as when standing in line.

Specifically, expectant waiting allows us to slow down long enough to observe what is going on within us. Thomas Kelly, in his book *A Testament of Devotion*, references two specific concepts that expectant waiting help reveal, the Inner Sanctuary and the Light Within, each of which has played an enormous role in my own practice of thanking and blessing.

> Deep within us all there is an amazing inner sanctuary of the soul, a holy place, a Divine Center, a speaking Voice, to which we may continually return. Eternity is at our hearts, pressing upon our time-torn lives, warming us with intimations of an astounding destiny, calling us home unto Itself. Yielding to these persuasions, gladly committing ourselves in body and soul, utterly and completely, to the Light Within, is the beginning of true life. It is a dynamic center, a creative Life that presses to birth within us. It is a Light Within that illumines the face of God and casts new shadows and new glories upon the human face. It is a seed stirring to life if we do not choke it. It is the Shekinah of the soul, the Presence in the midst. Here is the Slumbering Christ, stirring to be awakened, to become the soul we clothe in earthly form and action. And He is within us all.[1]

This, then, is why embracing expectant waiting is so wonderful—we can discover within us a place of stillness and balance, the Inner Sanctuary, where we can encounter the abiding presence of God, the active and guiding Light Within. Let's look at each of these more closely.

THE INNER SANCTUARY

A sanctuary is a sacred or holy place. In many religious traditions, the term is nearly synonymous with the physical structure in which believers worship. Indeed, in some cases the edifice is understood to be the very *house* of God. Yet the building itself is not special; it's the presence of the Divine in the physical place that makes it holy. Similarly, the Inner Sanctuary is a holy place. It is not a literal house for God, but it is a place where God meets us.

Practicing expectant waiting in order to discover the Inner Sanctuary may not be as easy as it sounds. First, you must stop distracting talk and diversions, and allow silence to envelope you. This can be a challenge in our modern world, for our culture seems increasingly fearful of silence. Televisions play in the background while we occupy ourselves with other activities in our homes. iPods and other portable devices pump constant stimulation into our ears, distracting us from being fully engaged with those around us. Cell phones interrupt movies, worship services, board meetings. Silence can be unnerving. So the first step in discovering your Inner Sanctuary through expectant waiting is to allow yourself to become comfortable with ... silence.

British Friend John Punshon writes a delightful description of his first attempt at worship through expectant waiting in his book *Encounter with Silence*. The setting was an unprogrammed Quaker meeting for worship, a type of service in which there is no planned program, music, or designated speaker. Individuals may speak briefly as they feel inwardly motivated to do so. As the group settled into worship, he found himself wondering what to do with the quiet. He wrestled with boredom, and fidgeted. He wondered what prompted a certain couple to marry. He even found himself contemplating the hair in the ear of the man in front of him.[2]

His experience is a common one, but different tactics can aid the transition to silence. Some describe it as an exercise of self-emptying, with a goal of becoming an unfilled receiver ready for any message God sends. In some contexts, using a simple chant or mantra can help. The use of images or words like "love" or "peace" in order to have a point of focus, especially when your mind begins to wander, is another common strategy.

In many respects, it is a matter of intentionality. At a weekend retreat I led, I used a guided meditation to help the group visualize their Inner Sanctuary. We sat in silence for five minutes or so, becoming aware of our breathing. A hush gradually fell over the group. People twisted and shifted in their seats, but as they continued to focus, their restlessness subsided. I encouraged them to visualize themselves sitting in their favorite place, comfortable and content. Next, I invited them to feel the spaciousness in this place. I reminded them to stay relaxed but intentionally focused on how their Inner Sanctuary was opening up.

At the end of the session, one person approached me and said, "I have sat in silence many times over the years, but this is the first time I have known what it means to be stilled within." That simple description captures the overwhelming effect of discovering the Inner Sanctuary. It is more than a mere place without noise. It is an internal condition in which our mind, our emotions, our inner rhythms are calmed to the point of stillness. There in the stillness, a numinous sensation arises within, signaling that we have reached holy ground where we can meet and be met by God.

Understanding that we each have an Inner Sanctuary, a place where we can encounter the Divine in a very personal way, empowers and transforms us. We don't have to visit a building (or go into nature, or go on pilgrimage, or go any*where*, for that matter) to find a place where we can meet God, for such a place is already within us. It is there that we discover, in Kelly's terms, the Light Within.

THE LIGHT WITHIN

Once we enter our Inner Sanctuary, we discover that we can encounter God there, for God dwells within us. This is sometimes called a theology of presence, and it is beautifully echoed in Psalm 139:7–8:

Where can I escape from Your spirit?
Where can I flee from Your presence?
If I ascend to heaven, You are there;
if I descend to Sheol, You are there too.

This is not only because God is in those places already; it is also because God travels there with us, in us.

That means that we can never be apart from God. We can still look to sacred texts, holy places, and communal rituals for meaningful experiences, but turning within for those kinds of experiences is just as valid. This has all kinds of ramifications. The Divine Presence dwelling in your Inner Sanctuary dethrones the power of religious authorities that threaten to deny access to the Divine unless you conform to their demands. Your relationship with the Divine does not depend on them or necessarily proceed through them. Indeed, the Inner Sanctuary demystifies the smoke and mirrors that some spiritual leaders invoke to restrict access to God.

So, once you reach the Inner Sanctuary, how do you encounter this Light Within? How do you discern it amid the tumultuous thoughts and conflicting emotions of your internal world? You do this by deepening your practice of expectant waiting to embrace silence. How exactly you achieve that depends largely on you.

For example, I happen to be a visual learner. One day as I struggled to deepen my practice of expectant waiting, it occurred to me that perhaps I was a visual worshiper as well, so I began to experiment during the silence with visualizing an encounter with God. I'm a Christian, so I imagined—naturally enough—meeting Jesus. With time, that mental picture changed to a visualization of me simply sitting in the Light—an image that is quite at home with Quakers, as it is with many other religious traditions. Then one day I became aware that in the deep meditative state that enveloped me, my mind was seeing colors that emanated from a pulsating center. It felt as though I were seeing the heartbeat of God. This was my Light Within.

More important than the particular image I used, however, was the movement that occurred from sitting in silence looking for aids to experience God, to a place where I was without question accompanied by Another. In that moment, I finally learned that there is a difference between being quiet and being settled. The former is about the lack of noise; the latter describes an inner disposition that has been soothed and calmed by God's presence. It reminds me of the words that appear in Exodus 3:5 when Moses encountered God in the burning bush: "Remove your sandals from your feet, for the place on which you stand is holy ground." This was an experience that in time has become part and parcel of the spiritual art I am describing, for it was a holy encounter that rooted me in God's original blessing and gave rise to profound gratitude.

Once I had my own experience of the Light Within, I suddenly wanted to engage in expectant waiting frequently. I wanted to return to my Inner Sanctuary and experience God's presence once again. I was willing to wait patiently until such time as I sensed the presence of God deep within my very being. For there at the intersection of the Divine and the human, I felt an incredible gratitude—for life, for the wonders of creation, and most of all for the conversation with God possible within my Inner Sanctuary. This gratitude was powerful, and as I returned to this practice over time, I found myself uttering words of thanksgiving and praise, both for the presence of the Holy One and for my connection with the whole of creation. This thanking interjected positive energy into my day, at the very least, and possibly into the wider cosmos, adding to the flow of God's blessings in the world.

This gratitude, and the eagerness to repeat the warm exhilaration I felt stirring in my soul, is not unusual. Once you experience it for yourself, you are no longer content simply to hear of another person's encounter, any more than you can be nourished by hearing what someone else ate for lunch. A significant part of the power is simply the experience of encounter—of being met—of inwardly feeling the reality of Holy Ground. This in and of itself can be overwhelming, but ultimately invigorating.

This is an experience of knowing and being known by God—an experience echoed in the Hindu concept of *darsan*, expressed in the fervent prayers of the Hebrew Bible, and affirmed by rabbinic spirituality that believes God may be encountered repeatedly. Listen and consider the experience of waiting to be met by God:

> Be still, and know that I am God! I am exalted among the nations, I am exalted in the earth. (Ps. 46:10, NRSV)

Or the experience of waiting for a manifestation of God's presence that will bring power and comfort:

> While staying with them, he [Jesus] ordered them not to leave Jerusalem, but to wait there for the promise of the Father. "This," he said, "is what you have heard from me; for John baptized with water, but you will be baptized with the Holy Spirit not many days from now." (Acts 1:4–5)

Or even the experience of power and transformation that comes through silent waiting:

> I myself am a true witness who came to receive and bear witness to the truth by being secretly reached by this life,

for when I came into the silent assemblies of God's people,
I felt a secret power among them which touched my heart,
and as I gave way unto it, I found the evil weakening in
me and the good raised up. (Robert Barclay, *Apology*)[3]

But this is not the end of the process. Ultimately, encountering
the Light Within transforms you in deep but gentle ways and
leads you back out into the world, guided by what I like to call
the Inner Witness.

THE INNER WITNESS

Once you come to a place where you are comfortable with
silence, and become convinced that within your Inner Sanctuary
there *is* the presence of the Light ... what next? If the Light
Within guides you, what does the voice of God sound like?
Without preacher, rabbi, imam, singer, or liturgy telling you
what God is saying, how are you supposed to know for yourself? Is it a thundering voice? Handwriting on the wall? In my
experience, it's been much closer to the experience of the
prophet Elijah, who discovered the voice of God in a most
unlikely way:

He said, "Go out and stand on the mountain before the
Lord, for the Lord is about to pass by." Now there was a
great wind, so strong that it was splitting mountains and
breaking rocks in pieces before the Lord, but the Lord
was not in the wind; and after the wind an earthquake,
but the Lord was not in the earthquake; and after the
earthquake a fire, but the Lord was not in the fire; and
after the fire a sound of sheer silence. When Elijah heard
it, he wrapped his face in his mantle and went out and
stood at the entrance of the cave. Then there came a voice
to him that said, "What are you doing here, Elijah?"
(1 Kings 19:12–13, NRSV)

Elijah did not discover God where you might have expected it—in the wind or earthquake. Instead, Elijah sensed God was present in the sheer silence. This invited Elijah to listen carefully, and when he did, God asked him a question that invited contemplation and introspection.

Another Friend named Isaac Penington penned these words describing his experience of the Holy:

> I felt the presence and power of the Most High.... Yea, I did not only feel words and demonstrations from without, but I felt the dead quickened, the seed raised, insomuch that my heart said, "This is He, there is no other: this is He whom I have waited for and sought after from my childhood." ... But some may desire to know what I have at last met with? I answer I have met with the Seed. Understand that word and thou wilt be satisfied and inquire no further. I have met with my God; ... I have felt the healings drop into my soul from under His wings. I have met with the true knowledge, the knowledge of life.[4]

Penington's idea of meeting "the Seed" is a perfect analogy for understanding the Inner Witness. It is an encounter with God, and contained in that encounter is all the potential and promise needed to inspire, influence, and guide future growth and action. Like a seed that gently unfolds into a sapling, the Inner Witness is often a gentle but relentless nudging, a still, small voice, a spark of initiative you may feel deep inside when you are practicing expectant waiting.

I certainly have experienced my Inner Witness in that way. There was the day that I nearly laughed out loud during silent worship among Friends. This was during a period of my life that had been filled with some significant and unpleasant surprises. I had begun to have some fundamental questions about my life's direction, including decisions I had made about my vocation.

Had I misunderstood God's direction? Had I chosen wisely? What was I supposed to do next? How could I resolve the dilemma I was wrestling with? On and on the questions came. But eventually, while I waited expectantly in this service, from the stillness of my mind the old Bible story of Ishmael emerged.

In that story from Genesis 21, Abraham had two sons: Isaac, the child of promise who arrived in Abraham and Sarah's old age, and Ishmael, the child born from Sarah's maidservant, Hagar. According to the story, Isaac was chosen as the recipient of the covenantal blessing, and Hagar and Ishmael were sent into the desert, where they nearly died. At the height of Hagar's despair, God promised her that her son would survive and, although he would live in perpetual strife, he too would be blessed by the blessing of Abraham.

That day, my mind heard the Inner Witness call me *Ishmael*, as if I, beset by troubles like Ishmael, also like Ishmael would be blessed and would ultimately prevail despite the efforts and decisions of others to thwart me.

I very nearly laughed out loud! The message, originating from the Light Within, illuminated some things about my own character that I needed to remember. But I also nearly laughed from relief, because it also contained an answer to my anxieties, and, through the nudging of my Inner Witness, I found the answer to my questions about what I should do. On top of that, I had a newfound appreciation for God's abiding presence and strength, and the blessings that were to come. All this left me with a profound sense of gratitude—of thankfulness.

But the Inner Witness doesn't always speak so softly. Not long ago I was about to embark on a months-long sabbatical and had made great plans to use that time for research and professional development. But something wasn't quite right. There were other signs, but the final piece came when I was traveling in France. When I tried to draw upon my college French, remnants of a single year of high school Spanish blurted out instead! These frustrating attempts led me to reflect on how valuable it would be to become fluent in Spanish, first as a resident of the United States, then as a leader of a school engaged in theological education, and finally as a member of a faith tradition with a small but vibrant Hispanic population in Central and South America. Very quickly, I realized a strong, internal push to learn the Spanish language and explore mutually beneficial relationships with Hispanic Quakers.

That internal compulsion led me to make new plans for my sabbatical—to travel to Central America, both to sharpen my Spanish and to build relationships there. One day, while staying in El Salvador, a pastor asked me why I was visiting his country. I answered in Spanish, "The *push* of the Spirit!"

What my limited vocabulary prevented me from saying was either "the nudge of the Spirit" or "the leading of the Spirit," either of which makes sense in a Quaker context. But really, in this case, "push" was more accurate, as my Inner Witness had shoved me out of my original plans and into others I hadn't ever considered before. I had felt pressed upon by the Other, of being grasped by an idea that would not relent until I submitted to its call.

These are just two ways that the Inner Witness operates within me, and the workings of the Inner Witness are different from person to person. Sometimes this engagement feels like saying yes to an intuitive hunch. In other moments it feels like a mental or an emotional oppression that churns within until I finally gain the clarity I need on the matter. However it works with you, it is that of God within that brings the Light to bear on the conversation of the day. It gives you a witness to the truth that you need to hear at that time. It offers the information that informs your next steps in the challenge of the moment. Always and in all ways it is an inner dialogue in which a Creator beyond total comprehension communes and communicates in a manner that conveys love, wisdom, guidance, assurance, and blessing. It never fails to move me.

Expectant waiting allows you at any time to retreat to your Inner Sanctuary, where you can converse with the Light Within, and receive guidance from the Inner Witness. This is a remarkable process, one that keeps you aware of God's blessing, and also fosters gratitude toward God because you find yourself in conversation, in worship, in dialogue, with the Creator in your most intimate of dwelling places. You see, hear, and feel the magnitude of divine love for you, and offer gratitude for the moment. This spontaneous act of thanksgiving is but one way in which thanking interjects positive energy into the course of your day, and possibly into the wider cosmos. In that way, your thanking of the Divine contributes to the ongoing flow of God's blessing in the universe.

EXPLORING THE INNER SANCTUARY

How and where do you look for God? You implicitly address those two important questions when you decide to engage in a spiritual search. You may go to distant holy lands or sacred shrines, or you may seek out renowned teachers, in your search.

By contrast, the sacred art of thanking and blessing redirects your attention inward. In the Inner Sanctuary of the soul, you learn to wait expectantly for an encounter with the Divine. In these meetings, God blesses you with a Holy Presence that, by itself, is reason enough to undertake the spiritual journey. As your skill at entering this inner dialogue improves, this Holy Presence becomes an Inner Witness that invigorates and offers you guidance. But it is a process that takes time, patience, and practice. Here are some suggestions for getting started.

A good way to commence reclaiming those blessed beginnings and a more tranquil pace of life is simply to sit silently. The very idea of this may generate a dozen objections, including the trump card in the deck—"it is a waste of time." If being silent is difficult, start small. Try to remain silent for fifteen minutes.

1. Wherever you are, sit comfortably and close your eyes. Take several slow, deep breaths. If any thoughts beg for attention, release them. As thoughts continue to spring up, don't give them any attention, and they will find their own way out.
2. Wait patiently. Listen expectantly. Hear the sound of nothing—it is amazing how overwhelming silence can be. It possesses a roar of its own.
3. When you are able to spend fifteen minutes in silence without feeling that you should be doing something else, begin to look inward. Pay attention to the rhythm of your breath.
4. Notice other sensations in your body. Imagine that with each inhalation the breath of God enters you. Feel the tingle of exhilaration as you become aware that God is within you.
5. If you are one who benefits from visualization, allow your mind's eye to visualize your waiting for God, being open to God's manifestation.
6. When you become aware of God's presence, sit quietly with it. Enjoy the moments.
7. If it feels permissible to do so, offer words of praise or ask questions that are relevant to your current situation.
8. Continue to wait quietly. Listen for the response of your Inner Witness.
9. Be attentive to sensations and impressions that well up within you. What images or thoughts come to mind? What feelings can you identify?
10. Tend to those sensations and impressions. What can you learn from them? How might they guide you?
11. If a feeling of gratitude and thankfulness emerges as a response to the presence of the Other, express it to that presence, or to those who enrich your life.

The practice of expectant waiting cultivates a sense of intimacy and immediacy with the Divine, and lets you experience the reality of divine blessing. Your Inner Sanctuary is a place of refuge where you can encounter the illuminating Light Within anytime, anywhere—even when standing in line at the airport. With time, you will recognize the Inner Witness as a reliable teacher and guide that is accessible at times other than in silence—indeed, it can help you maintain a nonanxious presence as you assess and respond to difficult situations.

As you cultivate this practice, feel the inner rhythms of your life synchronize with the eternal heartbeat. The resulting inner dialogue will communicate continued blessing from God. It will transform your countenance and fortify your confidence as you achieve clarity of your place and purpose in life and live out of this knowledge. And, it prepares you to think about how you carry your commitment to this sacred art into the public arena through the practice of sacramental living, which we consider next.

CHAPTER THREE

SACRAMENTAL LIVING

E xpectant waiting and the personal encounter with the Divine it encourages is a wonderful spiritual discipline that serves us well as long we take the time to practice it. Unfortunately, however, most of us cannot spend large blocks of time sequestered away in silence.

The good news is that the benefits of expectant waiting lead you into the next step of thanking and blessing—sacramental living, which allows you to encounter the Holy not just within your Inner Sanctuary, but out in the world in daily encounters, in every moment.

WHAT IS SACRAMENTAL LIVING?

Specific rites and rituals called sacraments, including marriage and Communion, have long been an important part of the Christian tradition. Specific understandings about the sacraments differ from denomination to denomination, but generally speaking, sacraments are considered to be visible signs of divine grace. Sometimes, the sacraments are even considered to actually confer God's grace upon the recipient.

I, however, prefer a broader definition that gets back to the original meaning of the Latin root *sacramentum*, "to make sacred." I like this way of thinking about sacraments because it is something available to each of us, regardless of our chosen spiritual path.

But what does it mean to make sacred? At its most basic level, to name something as "sacred" is to indicate that it is dedicated to God in some respect. In another sense, it invites us to look beyond the physical realm to a deeper, spiritual one where God can be known more clearly. A thing or an action isn't *just* a thing or an action—it also in some measure contains something of God, and if we have the eyes to see it, we can learn something new about God by looking deeply. This can become a way of life, what I call "sacramental living." Living sacramentally means becoming aware that every hour and minute and second we live is played out in the presence of the Divine. Sacramental living is akin to the Jewish commitment to *kedushah*—this is holy living. It happens when ordinary living is wrapped in the presence of an extraordinary, present God.

We begin to live sacramentally when we are able to acknowledge this Presence on a continual, or at least regular, basis, wherever we go. Holy ground is no longer limited to the area immediately surrounding the isolated burning bush or designated religious shrine. We experience God in our Inner Sanctuary, yes; but now we discover that we can experience God anywhere.

When you are in an office staff meeting that bores you to tears on Monday morning, try to remember that this could be holy ground—if you can discern, and respond to, God's presence there. If you grow impatient in the checkout line in the supermarket, remember that intentionally recognizing the Holy in that place can transform "wasted" time into a sacred moment—

perhaps by something as simple as engaging someone else in line in a way that cheers her day. When the merge lane of the highway or the heated disagreement with a friend threatens to drive you nuts, it may be helpful if you recall that these moments are bathed in the presence of God. Each is an opportunity to experience the sacred and to have that awareness leaven the moment with thanking and blessing.

There is a mystical quality to this, but you do not have to achieve the spiritual insights of a Desert Father or Mother to know God in this way. By mystical I mean simply an encounter with the Divine in which you feel swept up in an experience from which you ultimately gain knowledge and insight. This is far more than an intellectual exercise—it is a real experience that anyone can have, if you open up all of your senses to its possibility.

I recall an experience like this I had one night after class on a college campus. The class was a course in world religions. Coming from a conservative Christian tradition, I was wrestling with some of the ideas I was discovering in other religious traditions—ideas that appealed to me on a deep level, but were at odds with the teachings of my faith.

That night the class had been discussing the belief that all is One, and that appearances to the contrary are merely illusions. As I headed toward the parking lot, I began to feel dizzy. I felt my heart skip a beat. I seemed to shiver inside my own skin, and then, internally, I caught a glimpse of the reality that I, and the oak tree in front of me, and the red North Carolina soil beneath my feet, and the stars shining on that clear night, and countless unknown individuals in the community and around the world were all part of One. In a second, I saw and felt that I was part of a unity that encompassed all that is.

This wasn't a teaching or an idea. This was a real experience. It was a moment that offered an existential glimpse into the possibility that all is part of the same One.

But—now what? What was I to make of this new under-standing? It wasn't like I could walk away and pretend it hadn't happened. Objects were not just objects. Strangers were not completely strangers. The Divine, and us, and indeed everything that exists share important bonds, and my challenge was to sort through and integrate the significance of this new perspective, one shared by many faith traditions:

All that the Holy One created in the world, He created in man. (Talmud, *Avot de Rabbi Nathan* 31)

We shall show them Our signs in the horizons and in themselves, until it is clear to them that it is the truth. (Qur'an 41:53)

Where two or three are gathered in my name, I am there among them. (Matt. 18:20)

How Do You Live Sacramentally?

The new perspective I gained that night called for a new way of life, one that is continually open to more experiences. But how to start? A good way to begin living sacramentally is to make a con-scious effort to look beyond the surface of things and everyday situations. Evaluate on a deeper level.

Consider your own life. When you venture forth into public, you present a certain image. Yet there is so much more going on underneath. The casual observer may have no clue what unset-tling challenges you faced that morning—the subway delay, the lost wallet, the angry spouse, the crying child, the dying parent, the mid-morning meeting that has your stomach tied in knots, the toothache that haunts you, or the vacation that begins at the close of work today. Yet these are all components of your life. They are invisible mysteries to those around you, yet they affect how you present yourself and how you interact with others.

With this in mind, it's not so hard to imagine, then, all that you do not know as you pass persons on a busy street, as you answer the telephone call from a telemarketer, as you sit in the waiting area of the dentist's office. What's going on with them? What baggage are they carrying around, just beneath the surface?

Living sacramentally looks beneath the surface to ponder what could be motivating other people. It is engaged with what's happening at the moment, but it also understands there are emotional patterns and currents and unknown circumstances that are affecting every interaction you have, and it seeks to engage with the larger view of the scenario.

One day an irate person entered my office. He was so upset, and his expectations so unreasonable, that I felt my own anger rising, and I neared the point of yelling back with equal ferocity.

Then I felt a nudge from my Inner Witness, and suddenly I saw this man as an adult-size version of the five-year-old he once was. He was having an adult version of the temper tantrums he threw as a child. This was an old pattern that spoke volumes about how he acted when he was upset and needed attention.

When I realized that, all my impulses to defend myself or reject his arguments fell away and were replaced by a desire to respond with calm and warmth and genuine grace. Could I make space for him to reclaim himself so that the conversation could proceed along more productive lines?

You will never know all the dynamics present in a conversation or an encounter. However, sacramental living attempts to keep the larger picture of life as the backdrop against which this scenario unfolds.

COURAGE TO ENGAGE

When we have learned to be fully present and engaged in a situation and with the Inner Witness prompting us, the path of sacramental living needs only the courage to engage those we meet to contribute to the cosmic flow of thanking and blessing. The following chapters will offer more details on this engagement. For now, the emphasis is simply on our having the courage to engage.

This may feel a bit risky. As an introvert, I have to make a conscious effort to engage others. I have a colleague, however, for whom it comes naturally. Everywhere he goes, he speaks to people, regardless of whether or not he has ever met them before. He greets them. He engages them in conversation. He manages to find some way to connect with their current task, their interests, or their heritage. He also recently began taking Spanish lessons, and he is very creative in seeking opportunities to practice speaking it. He confessed to me that he even goes to the music section of a local store and lurks near the CD section where Latino music is sold, just so that he can initiate conversations with Latinos who come to shop for music.

Perhaps it is fearlessness. Or maybe it is the security that comes with knowing we are all made in the image of God and all connected to the One. Whatever the source of the courage, when we follow the sacred path of thanking and blessing, we discover ways to openly engage the world around us for the simple purpose of sharing in the creative work of God.

Not everyone will respond favorably, if at all, to our efforts. A friend of mine once greeted a person on the sidewalk with a typical Southern greeting of "How'ya doin'?" The stranger replied, "None of your damn business." That is not the response we would prefer, but the point of sacramental living is focused less on receiving positive feedback than it is on interjecting goodwill, blessing, and hope into the cycle of life.

ENGAGE THE MOMENT

The final step is to use that courage to gaze deeply into every encounter, confident in the knowledge that it holds the potential to be a sacrament.

One night around eleven o'clock, a telephone ring interrupted our peaceful evening. It was a wrong number. The person calling was an elderly woman looking for her son. She had had a yard sale at her home that day. It had ended hours earlier, but people were still coming by and entering her house unannounced, she claimed. She wanted her son to come put an end to this parade so that she could go to bed. Didn't I agree it was too late for people to be shopping at yard sales?

I explained to her several times that she had dialed a wrong number. Each time, she would acknowledge that, but then tell me the entire story again. I was tempted to hang up the phone, but it occurred to me that this was a sacramental moment. This person, created in the image of God, was disoriented. Maybe she had had a yard sale, maybe not. Perhaps people were entering her house, perhaps not. She would not tell me her son's name or the number she wanted to call. So, I listened to the story a few times. Each time, I asked her what she wanted to do next. She eventually offered her own solution in the form of a question: "Do you think if I just turn off the porch light and lock the door, people will stop coming in and I can go to bed?" Because she was calling from a small Midwestern town where there are no stoplights, very low crime, and the local police park a car with a mannequin by the town limits as a deterrent to speeding, I felt confident telling her that was a good idea. When we ended the call, I felt an internal joy that I had taken the time to be fully present in a way that treated with respect this person created in the image of God; I had lowered her anxiety, and, I believe, been a blessing in that moment.

If God created all, if there is that of God in all, if we are connected with all, then each moment holds potential for an encounter with the Divine. Those encounters are moments of deep communion with the Holy, and to some degree, the Oneness that unites us. These experiences grant new insights that allow us to create happier, healthier lives, and they teach lessons about engaging with and contributing to the world of which we are a part. These are moments in which we receive the blessings others offer, and moments to participate in God's work by being a blessing to them. Impulses to offer thanksgiving to God abound.

Such living begins simply by remembering that you stand as the image of God. When you awaken in the morning, remember that you carry the potential to have a positive influence on the day's activities. Your interactions each day can be the source of new insights and observations as God reveals creative possibilities about yourself and the projects you undertake. As you move out into the routines of life, go with the knowledge that the Creator is present all along the way. Making the morning coffee, commuting to work, conversing with colleagues in the elevator, even the prickly disagreement with a friend all occur in the presence and company of the Divine. Each moment, therefore, is potentially a sacred moment. Sacramental living lives and acts with some awareness of the fullness of time and the grandeur of the universe rather than with obsessive fascination with the outcome of the task at hand. In that present moment, you can serve and be served, you can learn and teach, you can witness and bear witness to the movement and leading of the Holy in that moment.

Could that be the experiential reality of the Shema's teaching from the Judaic tradition? It reads: "Hear, O Israel: The Lord our God, the Lord is One. And thou shalt love the Lord thy God with all thy heart, and with all thy soul, and with all thy might" (Deut. 6:4–5, JPS 1917 translation). Loving God with the totality of your being presumes that you know who and where God is. As you embrace the art of thanking and blessing, you discover a God who is more than a remote, outward, otherworldly deity; you know God indwells you, and you expect to encounter the Divine throughout the created order. With that in mind, you will need a love for God that is directed toward those expressions of God as well! Loving God as the Shema teaches enables you to bring love into those sacramental moments—holy moments—that fill your daily schedule.

THE LEAVEN EFFECT

Might sacramental living be the radical possibility contained in Jesus' teaching about the kingdom of God? "He told them another parable: 'The kingdom of heaven is like yeast that a woman took and mixed in with three measures of flour until all of it was leavened'" (Matt. 13:33). Jesus taught that God's reign was present and growing in the world. Like leaven in bread, this creative work continues to grow until it affects creation in its entirety. The whole loaf is transformed in the process—which is an amazing process to witness. I have seen institutional environments transformed when a commitment to consultative decision making replaced authoritarian, top-down management. Employees felt valued by the respectful environment characterized by compassion and grace. Upper management ceased to be a suspicious adversary. Everyone contributed their ideas to projects and supported the institution's goals rather than apathetically serving their time. All of this was achieved without lowering accountability or standards of expectation.

As you embrace the concept of an omnipresent, creating, blessing God present in everyone and everywhere, sacramental living helps you develop compassion and right attitude toward the whole of creation, nicely described via the image of a mother's love in this Buddhist text:

> Let none deceive another, or despise any being in any state. Let none through anger or ill-will wish harm upon another. Even as a mother protects with her life her child, her only child, so with a boundless heart should one cherish all living beings. (*Karaniya Metta Sutta*)[1]

In this mind-set, sacramental living brings abundant opportunities for you to bless those around us with presence, words, and kind deeds.

EXPERIMENTING WITH SACRAMENTAL LIVING

Sacramental living is the first step in the effort to participate outwardly in the continuing work of the Divine in the universe. In addition to the practice of expectant waiting, those traveling the path of thanking and blessing also expect encounters with the Divine in everyday affairs. This expectation reshapes the landscape of living, raising the stakes of casual encounters that might otherwise be dismissed. Life's journey is filled with opportunities to be touched by God, and consequently, opportunities to touch others on God's behalf.

FULLY PRESENT

One way to begin living sacramentally is to commit to being fully present where you are. We are a multitasking generation, which has certain benefits, but which may also stretch your attentiveness too thin. If this is the case, you may become distracted from the persons, tasks, or opportunities immediately before you. When you commit to being fully present, you penetrate the surface level of existence, where so much of your attention is focused, thereby missing many of the cues of deeper meaning.

- Pay attention to your surroundings!
- When you survey the countryside or cityscape, soak in the shapes and colors to the point of being awestruck by their complexity and beauty.
- When you go hiking, no matter where, hear the refrain "The earth is the Lord's and the fullness thereof, the world and those who dwell therein" (Ps. 24:1).

- Reflect upon what it means to see these places as God's places, and therefore as holy places. How does that change your perspective as you interact with your environment?
- When you make your rounds through the day, make a point of appreciating beauty. You can only appreciate beauty if you pause long enough to behold it—an advantage of being present in the moment.
- See the beauty of nature, whether lush and green or arid and barren.
- Admire the creativity of architectural design—whether it is in a chic downtown skyscraper, a modest ranch-style home, or a cardboard box that once housed a chest freezer but has been fashioned into shelter for a person with no other roof available. Consider the creative spirit that shaped each of these designs.
- Music plays a role in many formal religious settings in the form of hymns, choruses, and chants, but its ability to usher in holy moments is not limited to those settings. From the simple om of the Hindu and Buddhist mantras to the complexities of classical compositions and beyond, music has the capacity to move people in ways I can only describe as Holy Encounters. When music plays, do more than merely hear the melody— allow yourself to be moved by it.
- As you live sacramentally, give others your full attention when your paths intersect, however briefly.
- When encountering others, look at them. Acknowledge their presence. Listen deeply to what they have to say.
- Internally ask questions about value and meaning when events take an unexpected turn. What surprised you? Upset you? What might you learn in this instance?

ALERT SENSES

Though there is always more to life than meets the eye, there is much you can know when your life is sacramentally focused. When you live sacramentally, you utilize all your senses. It has been said that the eyes are the window to the soul, a sentiment I believe is not far from the truth. My two-year-old niece is a happy, smiling, energetic little child. She seems programmed for mischief, though, and her eyes give her away every time. Similarly, most of us recognize cues from the eyes, whether they are flashes of anger or light-hearted playfulness.

Sacramental living notices these cues and ponders them.

- What should you make of the blank, hopeless stare? Perhaps it is your signal that the person is preoccupied and needs a bit of encouragement.
- What does someone's hesitancy to answer contribute to your interpretation of the answer given? Perhaps the person is deeply considering his response, or perhaps she does not want to answer at all.
- What pain causes the nearly unnoticeable grimace of the person sitting across the table? You may not know the cause, but the grimace alerts you to the fact that all is not well, and this can shape your interaction with him or her.
- Does a person's extended arms and exposed palms invite you to continue your inquiry even though his words say he would rather not talk about it? Body language generally speaks the truth.

When you are attentive, you find many, many clues that help you better understand the flow of events that greet you each day.

COURAGE TO ENGAGE

If you are not ready to lurk near the CDs in order to speak with people, as my friend does, then try less aggressive steps.

- Learn to smile at those you meet. A smile sends an immediate signal that you are open to a positive encounter.
- Look people in the eye when you speak to them so that they may see the light and sincerity that you have for them.
- Practice small courtesies toward others—an easy way to help establish a warm, inviting context for engagement.

As you practice sacramental living, seek to determine what new lessons God is placing before you. Don't romp through the day without pausing to consider how you feel. Be attentive to your Inner Witness—what are your inner responses to these various encounters and situations? The Inner Witness can best guide you if you pay attention to the cues its raises within you.

- Are you eager to invest in the moment?
- Do you sense reluctance or even aversion toward an idea or activity?
- How do you feel about the next activity on your calendar?
- What do you think about the message the person in front of you is sharing?
- Is your mood altered as you complete a project or an encounter with someone else? Did you offer her grace and blessing? What did you receive from him? Where was the Divine quietly present in the interaction?

Through sacramental living, thanking and blessing flow in the respectful and compassionate exchanges with others. Respect and compassion yield incredible results. Why? We all appreciate being treated with respect, and we act considerately toward those who offer it. When life seems like one bad, rainy day, compassion helps you trudge along until the sunshine returns; you will likely reserve a soft spot in your heart for those who befriended you in your time of need and return the favor when it is needed. You give a boost to others when you offer respect and compassion.

Sacramental living turns your day into more than a series of loosely connected or disconnected events. It casts an aura of the Divine over the entire procession. It entices you to look for ways God accompanies you and guides you, sometimes playfully, sometimes profoundly. It prepares you to think carefully about how each moment is sacred. It even begins to influence your very disposition—a theme we consider in the next chapter.

CHAPTER FOUR

WALKING CHEERFULLY

The preceding chapters suggest that starting our story from the vantage point of divine blessing, cultivating the practice of expectant waiting, and learning the art of sacramental living will reshape our experience with the Divine. "Walking cheerfully" is the next step in the sacred art of thanking and blessing, for it calls us to a new level of commitment to this practice. More than being "on the lookout" for sacramental moments throughout our days, we can *initiate* them. When we do this, we discover that not only do we actively contribute to the flow of thanking and blessing in the cosmos, but also that the very manner in which we do it is mirrored back to us. In short, the more cheerfully we give, the more cheerfully we receive. Walking cheerfully helps build bridges between people, ideas, and even cultures. The more actively we engage the world around us with the intent to bless, the more open we become to its wonders.

WALKING CHEERFULLY IS TRANSFORMATIONAL

"Walk cheerfully over the earth, answering that of God in everyone." These eleven words form one of the most quoted sentences by a founding Quaker named George Fox. Such a concept might sound quaint, even naive, to our ears in this age of global terrorism and environmental decay. Yet, the Religious Society of Friends that formed around the work of Fox and others was birthed in England during the seventeenth century, a wildly turbulent time of political, economic, and religious unrest that threatened all corners of society. Far from being a pie-in-the-sky dreamer's slogan, Fox's words were a considered response to the greed, oppression, and violence of his day, challenges that rival our own four centuries later. He observed the human condition and the chaos of the times, and yet remained optimistic about the power of the human spirit, transformed by the power of Light Within, to rise above these circumstances.

One deep-seated frustration for Fox and others was the apparent obsession with religious ritual they observed in the Christian church. They deemed these practices corrupt, particularly because they did not see sincere spiritual transformation resulting from them. Fox rebelled against the Church of England, and in the 1640s he began touring the countryside, preaching that the church was more than buildings, that grace was not conveyed through rituals, and that faith should produce transformed lives. His journal describes mystical religious encounters in which he heard God speak directly to him—experiences that produced an eruption of internal joy as well as a set of new spiritual insights. In 1649 he wrote in his journal, "I heard a voice which said there is one, even Christ Jesus, who can speak to thy condition, and when I heard it my heart did leap for joy."[1] As a result of this and similar experiences, Fox arrived at certain insights that he chose to share through itinerant preaching and writing—practices that, in fact, modeled the sentiment of his statement: "walk cheerfully ... answering that of God ..."

Both "walking cheerfully" and "answering that of God" are important considerations that can deepen your practice of thanking and blessing. In this chapter, we will look closely at walking; in the next chapter, we will turn to "answering that of God."

THE WALK DESCRIBED

Fox's "walk cheerfully" phrase proves useful, beginning with the verb "walk." A growing number of spiritual disciplines use the literal act of walking in a variety of ways to encourage devotion and spiritual insight: through communal or individual prayer walks, walking the labyrinth, or going on pilgrimage, for instance. Walking is also a common metaphor for spiritual discovery: Many who search for truth refer to their "spiritual journey." In both cases, there is an implicit assumption that movement and progress are valuable, even necessary, in cultivating your awareness of the Divine in spiritual maturation.

But not everybody likes the image of walking. When I was in divinity school, a church history professor grumbled openly about "journey" imagery during one of his lectures. "Why does everyone emphasize the journey?" he asked. "Why do they all think I have to go somewhere in order to be holy? What if I like where I am? What if I don't really want to go anywhere?"

In some measure, that professor spoke tongue-in-cheek, but he made a good point. In spiritual terms, imagery and language of a journey can signify a sincere, intentional quest for truth and meaning. It can even give a spiritual raison d'etre to the wanderings of a nomadic spirit. On the other hand, it can collapse into a generic and overused label that merely disguises aloof detachment or disinterest in spiritual things.

I share that professor's complaint as a way of distinguishing the concept of walking cheerfully from more common understandings of undertaking one's spiritual journey. This kind of walking is not an endless exercise in navel gazing, nor is it a journey in search of something not yet discovered. Rather, it is an active response to that which we have *already* experienced—an awakening to our original divine blessing, the leading of our Inner

Witness, and the realization that every moment of life can be lived sacramentally. Walking forth is our way of mindfully engaging with the world with a commitment to contribute to the flow of God's blessing in creative ways. It is an intentional posture toward the world that is unafraid of the unfamiliar. It looks for good in a situation, and contributes positive thoughts and expressions to the encounter. It includes a spirit of discovery, as we shall see, and we ourselves benefit from this optimistic initiative. As the emphases of blessing—that is, goodwill and favor toward others—manifest themselves in our character, our own transformation can take cues from the insights of the Hindu and Buddhist concept of *ahimsa*, the goal of which is to eliminate human cruelty and replace it with cosmic love that is directed toward all creation. This is the spirit with which we venture forth.

This just might take the form of an actual walk undertaken to make a statement or gain attention. An example of one who walked cheerfully in the most literal sense is found in the legacy of Mildred Norman Ryder, a woman known to most only as the Peace Pilgrim. From 1953 until her death in 1981, she walked more than 25,000 miles across the United States. She vowed to continue walking until humankind learned the way of peace. You can still hear her joyous voice in audio clips found on the Peace Pilgrim website. There, her words communicate clearly her fervent commitment to her walk and to the ideals she committed to share. She had come to believe that knowing God created a love to be expressed toward all people and creation. According to the Peace Pilgrim, "To know God is to be so filled with joy that it bubbles over and goes forth to bless the world."[2] In short, she walked to bless people by her presence and her message.

But the walk might be much simpler than that—it just might be the everyday pattern of your life. It can be the path you follow in the routine of your day—the path that thrills you one day but may leave you exasperated the next. The key is to choose the manner of your routine so that it introduces blessing, so you are not simply gliding through the events of the day as best you can. As you practice the sacred art of thanking and blessing, designate your day-to-day journey as a walk to remind you that divine creativity and human initiative are partnered in every moment.

LOOK ALL AROUND YOU

One way to do this is to make sure that you keep your eyes open and continually (even literally) look all around you—not simply down at the ground, at your own path.

In a recent Spanish vocabulary-building exercise, I discovered the word for "firecracker" is *buscapies*, which literally means "looks for feet." The literal meaning prods me to wonder about the evolution of that word. My mind builds upon the idea—people with dispositions that look only downward, that is to say, "look for feet," disengaged from all surroundings except for the ground upon which they walk. This self-isolation can fester little firecracker-like explosions—such as anger, bitterness, loneliness, or selfishness—ignited by the constant disconnect between ourselves and the creation of which we are a part. If you feel isolated and alone, you may become angry with others for abandoning you, or with yourself for driving others away. Both the feeling and the rationale you attach to it may be completely wrong—a fact you will not likely realize as long as your eyes only "look for feet." In contrast to the downcast gaze, consider this teaching from the Buddhist text *Karaniya Metta Sutta:*

> With good will for the entire cosmos, cultivate a limitless heart: Above, below, & all around, unobstructed, without hostility or hate. Whether standing, walking, sitting, or lying down, as long as one is alert, one should be resolved on this mindfulness. This is called a sublime abiding here & now.[3]

In effect, the walk that looks upward and outward cultivates awareness of our surroundings. We do not live alone—therefore we are not destined to loneliness, nor can we be self-absorbed without consequence. These connections deepen our sense of self and our place in life, further stoking the fires of joy already ablaze from our relationship with the Inner Witness. Our senses better absorb the world around us when we look upward and outward—and our ability to live thankful, blessing lives benefits as well. The intensity of thankfulness builds as we encounter the Holy in the context of life's walk, and the capacity for being a source of blessing increases proportionally.

THE FOG

As we begin to actively seek ways of blessing others through our everyday encounters, we soon discover that not everyone holds the same ideas and opinions that we do! One way of making sure that as we practice the art of thanking and blessing we aren't imposing our own agenda on others, is to find and honor the common ground we do have with others.

This is not always as easily done as we might like. People of good conscience can disagree, sometimes vehemently, on any given topic. But in the art of thanking and blessing, even potential clashes of personalities or worldviews hold opportunities to manifest original blessing by building a bridge where there may not have been one before.

A strategy taught in some conflict-resolution seminars uses a technique called "fogging." It is tactic that teaches us to always find one item with which we can agree, however small, in the conflictual statements made by another. When we respond to that person, we lead with that item: "It is true that ..." This is the "fog" that precedes and makes space for less agreeable statements. It is a positive statement that builds a slight bridge, however tenuous, which may then, if necessary, be followed by a statement of a different point of view. Even in the worst moments of our day, when peace and joy threaten to elude us, the commitment to initiating blessing in our day is like the fog. It commits to finding some point of agreement or camaraderie that can be joyfully affirmed, even as it analyzes the rest of the scenario that must also be addressed.

But this is more than simply a useful negotiating tactic. This is a reminder that, however apart people may seem on any given issue, belief, or idea, we are each grounded in the same original, divine blessing. We all do, in fact, have something in common.

The Cheerful Disposition

Where does the walk take you? Wherever the Spirit leads! Judging from Fox's own travels, his language of walking "over the earth" could be taken quite literally. Your own walk may be less extensive, but still take you to neighborhoods and cultures that are not your own. Or you may barely leave the community where you were born and raised—it really depends on the life you choose.

Wherever you choose to walk, here is a thought to ponder: wherever you go, as you look upward and outward, the walk will introduce you to the great unknown! Stop for a moment to consider what it means to be one person in a world of 6.5 billion people. For all your familiarity with your family, your neighborhood, your culture, there is much about them that you do not know well. Imagine further how many other cultures there are in which your knowledge is seriously impaired. There is much to learn.

Life's walk takes you into unfamiliar territory. You can learn from those new experiences, especially if your disposition is one that cheerfully engages rather than avoids, hides, or, worse, demeans that which is different. As you take this journey, it is important that you learn, in Fox's words, to walk "cheerfully."

But what does that mean? Fox's adjective of "cheerfully" invites us to ponder the power of our own disposition in our routines, on those we encounter, and even upon our own fates.

I happen to be one of those people that is naturally cheerful. One evening as my wife, Judi, and I sat and talked I blurted out, "I am one of the happiest people I know, but I don't know why!" It's true. Most mornings, I awake in a good mood. There is often a song or melody already playing in the back of my mind. I don't know how it got there, but I, God, or someone greets me in the morning with a song. I leave the house anticipating that I will have a good day. The people in my office describe my laugh as infectious—once they even asked me to tape-record it so that when I am out of the office, my laugh will still fill the halls!

I seem to have always been this way. When I was a sophomore in college, a suitemate came into my room one night after I was asleep, turned on the light, and shook me awake. When my bleary eyes opened to focus on his curious face, I laughed out loud and asked, "What do you want?" His answer? "I just wanted to see if you were as happy in the middle of the night as you seem to be during the day. I thought for sure you would be mad." That is a true story. (I should add that my roommate was not amused by the late-night inquisition.)

But my optimism should not be mistaken for naivete. I know there are a lot of negative, even evil, transactions in the world. Even so, I love life and believe it is possible for love and justice to prevail. When I meet people, I expect kindness and honesty from them, and very often that is exactly what I get, even in situations where that might not seem likely. I believe this has a lot to do with the power of walking *cheerfully*—whether by natural constitution or by choice—because our moods and dispositions have power in the world. The way we receive and respond to others influences their responses, and is often mirrored back to us.

But in walking cheerfully, cheerfulness is more than a light, happy spirit, though that helps. When we walk cheerfully, we are open to exploration. We relish the encounter and engagement of the new and unfamiliar. Why? Because sacramental living has taught us that each moment is a potentially holy moment. Even the stranger or unfamiliar territory presents an opportunity to bless and be blessed. And if we are all part of One, shouldn't we make it a priority to know ourselves fully?

The important lesson to be learned from this is that the manner in which we engage the world influences, and sometimes determines, what we give as well as what we receive. Self-presentation shapes others' responses to you. A few years ago I was invited to co-lead a workshop with a person I had never met. Workshop participants had been identified as emerging leaders among Friends, and they were at the conference to talk about issues related to leadership and ministry.

As co-leaders of the workshop, we were to share our understanding of ministry, incorporating personal stories that described how we were called to this work. We are each white, North American males. Each of us was raised in an evangelical Christian tradition. My education included a liberal arts college education, followed by graduate work. My co-leader had attended a Christian college but had not attended seminary. Each of us enjoys rich ministries among Friends, and others view us as good, competent leaders. Though we were strangers, we had much in common, really. Our initial exchange of greetings was kind, but I detected a bit of suspicion in the co-leader's voice. It was slightly uncomfortable, but I chose to remain warm, kind, and open. We had only just met. Perhaps my read of the suspicion was wrong. After all, we were both created in the image of God, each had value, and we shared at least some common commitments. And, we needed to work together for the sake of this workshop!

During our presentation, I shared my surprise at feeling called to leave the family farm to pursue a path toward ministry. I described my sacrifices to put myself through college—financial stress; leaving the comfort of the community I'd lived in from birth; finding a new home for my pet; part-time, late-night jobs to earn spending money—but also the joy I experienced in helping others deepen their faith journeys. And, I reflected on my continued amazement at how life develops more wonderfully than my best-laid plans. I discover new joys, self-knowledge, and a sense of meaningful purpose through opportunities I never imagined. My current work as dean is one of them—I never desired the role, didn't think I would like it when invited to apply, and wasn't sure I wanted it after I interviewed. But it is the most rewarding work I have done up to this point in my life. In my opinion, I said to the group, this is a consequence of trying to live a life engaged with God and open to new experiences.

The co-leader shared next. He, too, offered a personal account of his move to ministry. What startled me, though, was a segue in which he acknowledged times when he formed opinions about another without having actually met the person. He said he thought God enjoyed putting him in situations where he was confronted with his own prejudices. In the middle of that confession, I realized that *I* was one of those persons. Our working together was, for him, the occasion of being faced with his judgments about me. We do, in fact, have several differences in our understanding of God and ministry, but my cheerful walk began to change the co-leader's opinion about me. The meeting provided a breakthrough moment where we were able to look beyond the surface and find our common ground. This is the kind of change that can come when we walk cheerfully—when we remain open and committed to conversation with those who appear to be different from us.

Walking cheerfully is highly practical. It allows us to encounter new situations with a sense of ease and humor on the one hand, and on the other hand allows us to remember that even as we act to increase the flow of blessing in the world, we continually receive blessings in turn, often as a result of the very kindness we project.

On a trip to Athens, Greece, I found that the city traffic resembled a clogged drain. Things moved slowly, with a good deal of churning and a lack of predictability. When I crossed the street I felt like I was taking my life into my own hands. More than once as I was caught in the middle of the street surprised by a car, I smiled broadly and raised an open palm to signal the vehicle to stop.

Later that evening, I learned that by raising my hand as I'd been doing all day, I had been insulting people's mothers all over Athens! I didn't know it, but the gesture I was using had an entirely different meaning in Greece than it did at home. But what really surprised me was that no one had shouted at me, accosted me, or even insulted me back.

Was this because I had raised my hand cheerfully—while smiling? Did that communicate that although I was a clueless tourist, I was at least friendly? Quite possibly. That, or perhaps those drivers just thought I was crazy and not worth the trouble of responding to in kind. Either way, I was grateful that no one had accosted me or escalated a situation I had no idea I had begun. I was equally thankful to learn how to be a better guest while in Greece.

I had another and potentially more troubling experience the night I arrived at the hotel on my first visit to Israel. After a grueling flight to Tel Aviv, followed by a lengthy bus trip to Tiberias, our group finally entered a beautiful hotel lobby. I was tired and thirsty and could barely stay awake. On a table, prominently displayed, was an ornate copper coffee pot. I began scouring the room for cups, cream, and sugar. Finally, when I politely asked where the coffee cups were, I was gently informed that that wasn't a coffee pot at all—it was a vessel used for ritual hand washing. And here I was trying to get coffee out of it!

In moments like that, I am grateful that my default disposition is one of cheer and openness. How easy it would have been for me to have been grumpy and demanding (after all, this was *my hotel*). What was an innocent misunderstanding could have turned into an embarrassing gaffe on my part, or worse, an insensitive insult to my hosts' religious beliefs. Fortunately, we were all able to laugh it off as the mistake that it was. As it was, both situations were educational moments for me. I became more culturally aware and respectful.

That is another advantage of walking cheerfully—it allows you to give yourself permission to make mistakes. In turn, this reinforces your ability to enter unfamiliar territory with an optimistic disposition, because your optimism does not depend on being correct—it is rooted in the expectation that you will encounter the unfamiliar but that new insights await you there. This allows you to be blessed, in turn, by learning about and receiving from new cultures.

Your walk does not have to take you to international locations for you to feel you are on foreign soil. When was the last time you knew exactly where you were, but felt well outside of your comfort zone? Was your disposition optimistic and engaging, or something else? My point is that this is not only a wonderfully created world; it is also a differently configured world. We live among different faiths, different family traditions, different local customs—each looking to create meaning, significance, and a smidgen of order in the rough seas upon which life sails. If you walk outside of your home (and maybe even if you do not), you have the grand privilege of experiencing another's world of meaning. The art of thanking and blessing invites you to engage with openness and be as mindful of your ignorance as you are confident of your knowledge. This helps you to better know when to speak and when to listen, when to offer and when to receive.

IT GETS EVEN BETTER!

Like nearly every conceivable realm of the human experience, disposition has fallen under the microscope of scientific inquiry, with intriguing conclusions. Certain research suggests that those with an optimistic disposition have better rates of recovery from surgery, have greater immunity, and are more resistant to high blood pressure.

Why is that? One hypothesis is that people with an optimistic disposition have clear and realistic boundaries—they understand the extent of their responsibility in any situation. That is, when faced with a negative scenario, they are able to identify and take responsibility for their role, if any, in bringing it about. At the same time, they are able to stop well short of assuming all the responsibility for it when that is not the case— they do not berate themselves unnecessarily or assume that they alone must solve the dilemma. They also possess a realistic perspective with regard to the permanence and pervasiveness of the situation as they interpret the past or anticipate the future. They do not see their current discomfort as an eternal sentence from which they will never be paroled. They believe life will improve, sooner rather than later.

These observations support the idea that you derive all kinds of personal benefit from a cheerful disposition as you undertake your spiritual walk. This cheerful disposition radiates from your experience of God. It is joyful because it is genuine. It is positive, but also realistic. For instance, I have high regard for human potential and expect decent, fair treatment from others. That is a positive, even gullible, view. However, I know that not everyone I meet will necessarily treat me kindly or fairly. That is realistic. I enter every new relationship with that hope and expectation, but if my hope is not realized, my high regard for humanity is not jeopardized by that one encounter—I am optimistic, but not utopian.

The cheerful walk is a walk that understands Jesus' teaching regarding the lilies:

> Consider the lilies, how they grow: they neither toil nor spin; yet I tell you, even Solomon in all his glory was not clothed like one of these. But if God so clothes the grass of the field, which is alive today and tomorrow is thrown into the oven, how much more will he clothe you. (Luke 12:27–28)

Jesus' words encourage us to understand the depth and magnitude of divine care for all of creation. When you see how true this is, many of your impulses toward fear and suspicion vanish, which makes the cheerful walk possible. Walking cheerfully is more than a playful gallop through life or a star-struck contemplation of nature. This is a confident trust that provides the courage to walk among the pathways of your life, knowing that the Divine Presence accompanies you and will meet you and greet you all along the way. This is true whether you are walking in familiar or unfamiliar terrain.

EXPERIMENTING WITH THE CHEERFUL WALK

It's easy to begin learning how to walk cheerfully.

1. Begin by sitting quietly in preparation for your day. Visualize your day's itinerary as an intentional journey, not a task list. View the activities as your contribution to the ongoing work of God's creative spirit. See your day as one means in which you offer thanks to God and share the blessing of yourself with your corner of the world.

2. Work to cultivate a positive disposition within yourself. Over your morning cup of coffee or tea, remember some of the best and worst days of your life. Recall the mental and emotional states of being that dominated those experiences.

3. Reflect on how those states of being caused you to act, and to interact with others. Negativity allowed to roost in our hearts poisons our attitude. It alienates those around us. It complicates our ability to walk cheerfully.

4. Identify your hurts and needs that enjoy nursing the negativity. Carry them into your Inner Sanctuary. Seek the healing and wholeness you need.

5. As you walk through the day, meet the world with welcome engagement. When distractions divert your attention, remember your commitment to cheerful encounters, and allow that choice to influence your disposition. What do you have to offer in each situation? What can you learn or receive from each experience?

6. Consider your impact. A decision to walk or not to walk, to go cheerfully or not cheerfully, is a decision with an impact upon others. A cheerful disposition buoys others when they encounter you. You influence them when they witness the radiant joy that fuels your enthusiasm. Appreciation may lead to admiration, which, with a little luck, may become emulation. In the words of another Friend, William Penn, "The virtue and efficacy of this Light for the end for which God hath given it is to lead and guide the soul of man to blessedness."[4] As your cheerful walk shares blessing, blessing returns to you as well.

Walk cheerfully over the earth. It is one way you put sacramental living into practice. You not only expect to encounter the

Divine throughout the day, but you also actively work to introduce blessings in your walk. An open, cheerful disposition grows from your experience of being richly blessed. It, in turn, is a means by which you bless the world.

Perhaps it is nothing more than offering a smile or lending a listening ear. It could include crossing cultural divides with grace so that stronger bridges are built. Or it could be learning to fog in moments of disagreement—finding something of value without condemnation, even as you prepare to articulate your disagreements. Walking cheerfully does your own heart good— and it invites others to respond in ways that add blessing and gratitude to the universe's grand flow. And, it prepares you for the next step in this sacred art, described in the next chapter— answering that God in the other.

ANSWERING THAT OF GOD

Airports are the Rodney Dangerfields of public transportation systems. They get no respect. Long lines. Lost luggage. Overpriced parking. Those irritations make many travelers' short list of top travel frustrations. I also have experienced all of those things, and still, I think airports are one of the happiest places in the world. Why? Because of the scene I have witnessed played and replayed at every airport I have ever been in. From the arrival lounge just outside of security, through the baggage-claim area, to the sidewalk outside, friends and loved ones rush to one another in a flurry of warm greetings. Some of the biggest smiles, deepest hugs, and most exuberant joy I have ever witnessed happened at airports. In those moments, I have witnessed the power of reunion.

When I was a child, whenever my aunt from California visited, the whole family would travel to the airport in nearby Greensboro, North Carolina. In those days, we waited on the rooftop of the airport and watched planes land, until finally Aunt Martha arrived. By the time she got off the plane, we were all so giddy with anticipation, you would have thought she was a Hollywood celebrity. Everybody was absolutely joyous, and she was just as excited to be greeted by such a friendly mob.

FIRST IMPRESSIONS, OR REUNIONS?

Reunions are a helpful way to continue exploring the sacred art of thanking and blessing. From a spiritual perspective, since we are all made in the same image of God, all meetings are reunions of sorts—a gathering of folks who share a certain connection.

When my family comes together around holidays, it includes not just my immediate family but also extended kin, including cousins, significant others, and even pets. In my family, that usually means dogs. While we human family members spend time getting reacquainted, what I really enjoy is watching the dogs meet and greet each other. If you own a dog, you know exactly what I'm talking about. When dogs come upon a new place or another strange dog, they immediately survey the situation and clarify the pecking order. How? They sniff each other. Not very subtle, to be sure, but I admire the fact that this species has an open, predictable means for navigating those first, sometimes awkward, moments of encounter.

People aren't as obvious about it, but don't be fooled. We do size one another up! What happens when we meet someone we don't know? In a flash, and often without even being conscious that it's happening, we make an evaluation based on our first impression. Who is he? Do I like her? Is he like me, or different? Good looking? Ugly? Those impressions are based on our internal set of values and prejudices.

These evaluations bear directly on how we treat those people. If the first impression is favorable, we might smile and even offer a handshake or a hug. We will be more disposed to listen sympathetically, share of ourselves openly, even offer help or assistance in some way. On the other hand, if our first impression is negative, we may engage the person coolly, send discouraging body-language signals, or even try to get out of the room. The first impressions we have of people are incredibly powerful.

Unfortunately, our first impressions are often superficial and based more on our own assumptions and prejudices than on anything actually to do with the person. When we are immersed in the practice of thanking and blessing, our Inner Witness will begin to challenge those knee-jerk decisions and discouraging mannerisms, because it is teaching us to be more perceptive and discerning when we encounter others. We are embracing a perspective that enjoys new discoveries, and that includes people. As we approach others in the spirit of living sacramentally and walking cheerfully, we will naturally begin to look beyond our first impressions, genuinely engage others, and get to know them for who they are, not who we think they are.

SEEING THAT OF GOD IN EVERY PERSON

Once you accept the idea that humans are created in the image of God, it is not a great leap to recognize that there is "that of God" in each person. Quaker spirituality takes this to another level by building upon the idea contained in the second part of the George Fox quotation introduced in the last chapter. "Walk cheerfully over the earth answering that of God in every person." Sacramental living prepares us to look for God in every moment. Cheerful walking instills the open, optimistic demeanor that bravely proceeds into unfamiliar places. "Answering that of God" focuses specifically on seeing every other person as a child of God, equally valued; it works to connect and develop a relationship at that deepest, spiritual level. This is the practical implication of Jesus' description in the Gospel of John. Described as the true light, Jesus is portrayed as the one who "enlightens everyone" (John 1:9).

This is more than theoretical. As you learn to sense the movements of your Inner Witness, you will discover that the same Inner Witness abides in others as well—even if it's not obvious at first. This is the moment when the sacred art of thanking and blessing emphasizes what has been implicitly obvious to this point: what is true about God's presence to and within you is equally true of God's presence to and within others. This is more than a glib theological statement. It has profound implications for the most basic of social interactions. A life of thanking and blessing offers great benefit to those who embrace it, but it also makes certain demands upon you as well. This is one of those times, but even this is mutually beneficial!

Several years ago, I served as a pastoral minister for a Quaker meeting. "Meeting" is Quaker terminology for "church." We did not engage in overt evangelism or proselytizing, but we comprised a striking theological and economic diversity, and we were an inviting and welcoming group. Attending one particular Sunday was an elderly man whom none of the members recognized. He entered quietly and selected a pew in the middle of the room. His clothes were not typical "Sunday clothes," and he appeared a bit haggard. From the front where I sat, it was apparent that people had moved quietly away from him. Later that week, a well-dressed businessman stopped by my office to ask me what we were going to do about the man. I asked him what the problem was. "Well," the businessman said, "he lives in an abandoned bus in a pasture of goats, and he smells to high heaven. What are we going to do if he returns?" In what may or may not have been my brightest moment of counsel, I answered simply, "We should invite him to stay for coffee. That's what we do with anyone else who visits here."

How do we assign value and merit to people—by the appearance of their clothes? Any religious tradition worth its salt sees beyond such superficial valuations. But the questions remain: how do we determine if the person standing before us is worth our time? You and I make those decisions every day. On what do we base those decisions?

Words like these from the prophet Isaiah discourage us from leaping to superficial conclusions on these matters:

No, this is the fast I desire:
To unlock fetters of wickedness,
And untie the cords of the yoke
To let the oppressed go free;
To break off every yoke.
It is to share your bread with the hungry,
And to take the wretched poor into your home;
When you see the naked, to clothe him,
And not to ignore your own kin.
Then shall your light burst through like the dawn
And your healing spring up quickly. (Isa. 58:6–8)

Through the prophet, God challenged the people's participation in religious rituals such as fasting while ignoring injustice, hunger, and poverty. This type of disregard is only possible when the just, the well fed, and the rich depersonalize the needy—that is, fail to see that of God in the other. If we knew God were hungry, we would offer food. If we discovered our friends were naked, we would assist them. And yet, it seems a perennial challenge for us to feel the same urgency when it is a supposed stranger in need.

This particular man did return and became a regular attendee. His story, once we heard it, was heart-wrenching, and he was quite likeable. He never once came to worship when he didn't wear the strong smell of goat, though he did start to comb his hair from time to time!

Most of us can cite an incident like this one. It is where the path of thanking and blessing acquires a bit of an incline. It is not a difficult thing to believe that there is that of God in every person when the person is likeable, especially if he or she is "like us." When that belief requires us to step outside our comfort zone, our skin may crawl. In times like that, we will need to take a deep breath and step out of the zone.

Sometimes, our insensitivity is less overt. Several years ago, I attended a community forum on the subject of racism. The town had a population of about 18,000 and had one of the strongest community spirits of any place I have ever lived. Of those 18,000, about 500 were African American. During that discussion, some people spoke in favor of tolerance of those who were different. It was the kind of remark that drew immediate nods and affirmations, but not for long. With a calm, nonthreatening voice, a middle-age black woman set us all straight when she said, "I have been tolerated in this town all my life. I have to tell you—I am tired of being tolerated. I want to be accepted." To my knowledge, she had not been actively persecuted or hated by anybody in that town, but the spirit of separation was still prevalent, and she knew it. She *felt* it, daily. Some still found it difficult to accept or love her as she was. When you engage in a path of thanking and blessing, your Inner Witness will actively remind you day in and day out—when you answer that of God in *every* person, skin color or ethnicity does not matter any more than the clothes you wear.

Jesus' teaching pushes us even further on the issue. Among the many difficult teachings of Jesus in Matthew 5 is this one:

> But I say to you, "Love your enemies and pray for those who persecute you, so that you may be children of your Father in heaven; for he makes his sun rise on the evil and on the good, and sends rain on the righteous and on the unrighteous. For if you love those who love you, what reward do you have? Do not even the tax collectors do the same? And if you greet only your brothers and sisters, what more are you doing than others? Do not even the Gentiles do the same?" (Matt. 5:44–47)

This is a hard teaching to swallow. These words insist that the higher way includes loving—not merely acknowledging or being pleasant to—but loving people who do not have your well-being in mind.

It Takes Patience

A few years ago, many people enjoyed a fad called "Power Vision" or "Magic Eye." I was not one of those who enjoyed it. These clever pictures are composed of bits of color, sometimes arranged in abstract patterns, sometimes not. They might even pass as elementary-school abstract art projects.

These caught on like wildfire. Soon they were appearing as framed photographs hanging on walls in public places and as a feature in the Sunday comics. The novelty and attraction of these pictures was that, if you stared at them long enough and relaxed your eyes in just the right way, a 3-D image would slowly emerge from the apparent two-dimensional chaos of the colors. It was kind of like a picture within a picture that slowly gained depth and form. Or at least that is what they tell me. I have never actually seen a 3-D image, though not for lack of trying. My sister gave me an entire book of these for Christmas one year. I have yet to see the first picture within the picture. It is like having a present you can't unwrap.

Seeing that of God in every person is like a Power Vision exercise. To succeed, you need the ability to gaze at people long enough to see past their outer shell with all its trappings and distractions, and into their soul where you see them as they truly are. Beyond the clothing, the skin color, the hairstyle, the ethnicity, the body art, the favorite hobby, the race, the favorite food, the religious affiliation, the education level, the indifference or even ill will toward you—you hold your gaze firm until those categories fall away and you discover that of God in another person.

This isn't easy, but once you have seen them in that light, you will be hard pressed not to respond to their need. The prophet Isaiah said it would be at that point that your light bursts forth and your healing arrives. And, that is where the reunion begins. For at that point—and not a moment before—you understand that every encounter, whether with friend, foe, or stranger, is at heart a reunion. If you share in being created in the divine image and are part of One, the other is not completely separate, stranger, or other; you may be very different, but you are also kindred spirits.

At a most basic level, the realization that there is that of God in every person is a lesson about kinship and reconciliation. Kinship, for obvious reasons; reconciliation because without acknowledging your kinship, you are as estranged as the brothers Jacob and Esau in the Genesis story, where Jacob cheats Esau out of his blessing and inheritance. Their common bonds were buried deeply beneath layers of suspicion and mistrust, until the day they could finally recognize the divine blessing evident in the other and were able to reconcile. Likewise, unity and healing can occur in your family and community when you acknowledge that of God in the other, which leads to reconciliation.

IT TAKES ATTENTIVENESS

Amazing things are shared—both given and received—once we recognize that of God in the other. Barriers that formerly separated us lose their divisive power. Status symbols become irrelevant. The playing field of life levels. We are humbled, yet lifted up, now capable of discovering the uniqueness, the wonder, the splendor, and the value of the other, and a new world of possibilities opens before us.

A fresh example of this rests with me. During a recent worship service, a guest quartet offered two songs during the morning worship. Even as their first words registered with my mind, I relegated the group to the background, just like I do when commercials interrupt a television program. But my Inner Witness gently nudged me, reminding me that these people, these strangers, had that of God within them. They had come to offer gifts to the morning's experience. By tuning them out, I was cheating myself out of a blessing.

So my mind reengaged the quartet. I looked into the face of each one. I listened to their harmonized tones. Their words were inviting me to worship on a deeper level. Suddenly the piano music came alive as well, gift-wrapping words, harmony, and expressions into a holy unity offered to me. Within my chest, a warm feeling grew, and I knew these four strangers had ushered me into a holier moment than I was having on my own.

People we hardly know will introduce us to many of the richest, most satisfying experiences of our lives. The key to receiving the blessing begins with acknowledging their inherent value as individuals, followed by attentiveness to what they are sharing. This perspective raises the stakes of sacramental living even higher. This is no longer just a saunter through life in hopes of God-sightings that bring warm moments. This is recognition of the value inherent in all things because of their place in the created order. It is part of the creative process that reunites that which has been estranged. It is an expedition of discovery.

One of the most profound gifts we can give to one another is the simple acknowledgment of this truth about each other: you carry that of God within you. Your life is sacred because of this, and you deserve to be treated with respect and dignity. That becomes our pledge to one another.

ANSWERS ENCOURAGE US

There is one more thing to be said about the idea of "that of God in every person." The phrase "Walk cheerfully … answering that of God …" includes a verb: *answering*. In my own faith tradition, this verb is frequently dropped, reducing the concept to a value statement, however important it may be. By rejoining "answering" to the phrase, it becomes an action statement. It calls for a response on the part of the spiritual pilgrim. We can theoretically understand the value and worth of others, but this is acting at a distance, which short-circuits the art of thanking and blessing. When we "answer" others, we move beyond merely acknowledging their value; we intentionally speak to the heart or spiritual core of those we meet. We connect at the level of our most common ground. Our answer acknowledges their worth, but it also invites them to begin a relationship with us that is grounded in our spiritual commonality. Because we treat them as the children of God that they are, we encourage, if not challenge, them to live up to and out of their potential. Answering that of God should set off a chain of reverberations within those who hear the answer, causing them to rise up to their own capability.

I recently stopped by a home-builders supply store on my way home from the office. It had been a long day, and my energy was sapped. I grabbed the two items I needed and looked for the shortest checkout line. I paid for the articles, and as I waited for my change the cashier looked at me and said, "You're a minister, aren't you?" To this day, I don't know why she thought that, or asked me about it. What I do recall is that in the midst of my fatigue from the day and preoccupation with the project I intended to work on at home, I was not paying attention to who and what was before me. But her question spoke directly to my core. Who am I? What am I? How am I representing that in this particular moment? Her comment called me to attention!

EXPERIMENTING WITH ANSWERING

This part of the sacred art of thanking and blessing is nothing less than a spirituality of discovery. We discover a common unity. We discover an extended family. We discover a beauty that transcends our differences. We discover how wonderfully rich and creative we all are. We discover there are a multitude of blessings to be received once we are aware of the One who offers them. And together, with this vast array of gifts and goodness, we discover a much greater set of possibilities before us than we ever previously imagined.

Here are some activities to help you begin reaping the benefits of the reunion:

- Consciously remind yourself that the people before you have that of God in them. How does that change your perception of them?
- Think of the person whose presence stirs the greatest degree of consternation within you. Despite whatever justifiable reasons you can offer for disliking this person, when you practice expectant waiting, imagine this person being held in the Light of God. Hold him or her there until, like the Power Vision puzzles, you see that of God in the person. How does this person look in this Light?
- Find at least one quality you have in common with this person, and one quality that you can celebrate when you next meet that person. When you see this person, commit to building on this trait.

A second way to live this new understanding is to have the courage to seek the thoughts and opinions of others. If a decision is yours to make, you give away no power by asking for advice. On the other hand, you open the door to a potential storehouse of wisdom. Others may approach a situation differently. They may think outside the box, or inside a different box than you do. In either case, listening to the ideas of others is a powerful gift to all parties, even if you decide to act differently than they recommend. Experiment with this.

- Invite others into your circle of activities.
- Ask for their advice.
- With this simple gesture, you demonstrate their worth and your respect in ways that will strengthen the relationship you have with them.

As you build these relational bridges with others, do not be surprised if they, in turn, begin to value your opinion. When that happens:

- Offer honest but caring input.
- Speak in ways that affirm the value of the person, but also that resonate with the leading of your Inner Witness.
- Expect to see the quality of these relationships change. Interaction of this depth cultivates genuine, spiritual friendships grounded in love, trust, and integrity. One cannot ask for a truer foundation of friendship.

These simple steps will change your environment and your interactions for the better. Be sure not to overlook these changes. At the end of each day, at least in the early stages, do the following:

1. Spend a brief period of time in reflection.
2. Think about where you saw God throughout the day.
3. Give thanks for each of those sightings.
4. Consider what new gifts and qualities you observed among those with whom you reunited. What surprises did you experience? Give thanks for those surprises and the accompanying knowledge that came with them.
5. Reflect upon how your world is expanding, becoming a much friendlier place to walk, as you see God in others. How is this changing your outlook on life?
6. Consider where you were able to be a blessing to others this day as you "answered" that of God in

others. This is a two-way street. You, too, have much to offer others on their journey.

Remember to rejoice and give thanks. Each day this is practiced, the quality of your spiritual insight improves. As you answer that of God in others, the quality of the world's activities is improved, and you give others a boost they may not have even known they needed.

CHAPTER SIX

THE AMBIANCE OF LOVE

I think everyone wants to love and be loved, because love is powerful. It is a potent mixture of emotion and will that creates incredible resolve and commitment. It can change the mood of the moment, and even transform an environment. We feel incredibly valued and safe when we receive love. When we give love, we enjoy the ability to make another person smile or encourage them to fulfill their dreams. Together, we strengthen and encourage each other with a mutuality of care.

Sometimes, love surprises us. It moves us to have affection for people we did not intend to care about. I have a friend who, with every ounce of her strength, resisted falling in love with the man she eventually married until finally she could only accept the attraction that stirred so deeply within her. Love prompts us to sacrifice things we want for ourselves because we would rather improve the quality of someone else's life than provide for our own gratification. We can probably all remember a pair of shoes or a week at camp where, for the sake of our needs or dreams, our parents simply did without something they needed in order to provide for us. From wedding vows to prison visits, love, or the desire for it, motivates the commitments that keep us invested in each other's lives.

One of our greatest discoveries on the path of thanking and blessing is that love is already within our reach. Love surrounds us as completely as the air we breathe. It is a quality of God's fundamental attitude toward us. It is a mysterious and powerful force that, once experienced, can change our lives radically, heal wounds, eradicate fears, and shape the words and deeds that we offer to the world. The love that flows from us in turn affects those around us, and we continue to participate in the ongoing, creative work of God.

LOVE AND GOD

The sacred art of thanking and blessing builds upon the conviction that humans are created in the image and likeness of God, and that God's image and likeness take form in our lives. But what is God like? Many religious traditions understand love to be one of God's fundamental defining characteristics.

A common refrain in the Hebrew Bible describes God this way: "The Lord! The Lord! a God compassionate and gracious, slow to anger, abounding in kindness and faithfulness, extending kindness to the thousandth generation ..." (Exod. 34:6–7). It is a description I cherish, in large part because of the Hebrew word *hesed*, translated here as kindness. "Steadfast love" is another common translation, though that fails to capture the power and depth of the word. *Hesed* is the quality of love that inspires trust and confidence in the face of adversity and peril. It is a tenacious love, a love at the core of God's covenantal commitment to God's people. *Hesed* assures us that God has our best interests at heart.

Islam underscores the priority of love in the divine nature, referring to *ramah*, or love, as God's normal attitude toward humanity: "O our Sustainer! You embrace all things within love and knowledge" (Qu'ran 40:7). It is a patient, kind love, designed by Allah and beyond our complete comprehension.

Christianity equates God and love, as explicitly stated in 1 John: "Beloved, let us love one another, because love is from God; ... for God is love" (1 John 4:7–8). Both the New Testament and several early Christian writers describe this love as *agape*, by which they mean an unconditional, nondiscriminating, self-giving love. Moreover, the New Testament understands Jesus as the ultimate example of this self-giving love that God offers to humanity. In turn, this love becomes the motivation for humans choosing to love others.

In short, God and love are inseparable from each other, as are humans from God's love. Few statements surpass the New Testament conviction of Romans 8 on this matter:

> For I am convinced that neither death, nor life, nor angels, nor rulers, nor things present, nor things to come, nor powers, nor height, nor depth, nor anything else in all creation, will be able to separate us from the love of God in Christ Jesus our Lord. (Rom. 8:38–9:1)

We are inseparable from God's love. That is an inviting concept, but how are we to think about this love and its effect upon us? After all, love has a funny way of working. It's not always logical, or direct, or even easily identified. I have come to think of love as a kind of ambiance in my life—something that's real, and powerful, but not simple to pin down. Just like the effects of lighting create an ambiance in a room—low, soft light for a romantic dinner, or bright, colorful lights for a party—love's glow affects perception and mood in sometimes subtle, yet very real, ways. It can shape your attitude. It can electrify your whole being one minute, and then fill you with profound gratitude the next. Love leaves us thoroughly undone but wonderfully remade.

When I was thirteen years old, I experienced a transforming encounter with the ambiance of God's love during an annual series of revival services in the evangelical Friends meeting I attended. While the pastor spoke, my heart felt a burning presence of God. I felt emotionally vulnerable and undone. I knew I was being called to a new life—a conscious, intentional journey of faith. The pastor invited those who wanted to respond to God's love to come forward to the altar for prayer. I didn't want to take the first step or make such a public display in front of all those people. But it didn't matter. I couldn't resist. I made my way forward, not certain what I was doing or even why—only that I couldn't *not* go up. With words of prayer, I offered myself to God that night. Immediately, I felt a sense of relief and release, as though I were indeed a new person.

A few days afterward, my mother remarked that she knew something genuine had occurred. "How?" I wanted to know. She replied, "I see it in the way you treat your sisters now." These were my early teen years, and I was a typical big brother. I was not really mean, but I confess that I did enjoy tormenting my siblings. To this day, all three sisters insist that they flinched when I passed by in the hallway, bear scars from my various nicknames for them, and can cite half a dozen stories that leave me speechless from embarrassment. What exactly I encountered at that meeting is still difficult to describe adequately, but the ambiance of love had worked its way into my soul and changed my feelings for and actions toward my sisters.

Now and again I pause to remember that exchange with my mother and to acknowledge that the change she observed was genuine. I believe that encounter with God healed some wound within me that I scarcely knew existed. I no longer needed to tear others down merely to build myself up. My experience is not unique. As I talk with others about their experiences of divine love, they confirm the positive, healing, even transforming effect that divine love brings to their lives. A friend of mine remembers feeling his heart warmed when he was five years old. He shook in his seat during a gathering for prayer, and actually stood to pray aloud—much to his own surprise and that of the adults in the group. I know people who can remember an exact time when they knew they were loved fundamentally and wholly. I know others who describe realizing this truth slowly over the course of their life's journey. On the other hand, I know others who are still searching for this realization.

If God is love and humans are made in the image of God, then our learning to love is a theological imperative. More than that, it is our invitation to step into that image by consciously imitating the divine love we experience and radiating it out to others. In the process, love provides perpetual energy for thanking God, transforming our abilities to engage others, and blessing those around us.

WHAT DO WE KNOW ABOUT LOVE?

Learning to love begins with reexamining our understanding and experience of love, especially with regard to God. It seems that whatever capacity for pure love we may have possessed when we were born is smudged pretty quickly. The earliest lessons we learn about love come from parents and caregivers. Even with their wonderful attributes and good intentions, through no fault of their own they may have had flawed understandings of love. As they taught us, our understanding of love became entangled with the expectation of rewards and favors. At times, we received subtle messages that love would be withheld if we did not meet certain expectations. Perhaps we even came to view God this way, too, as one prone to withhold favor or even issue judgment if we did not live up to certain standards. In turn, this became the kind of love we knew how to give, to both God and others—love as an effort to cultivate acceptance, receive favor, and even manipulate others for our own purposes. And if we didn't get what we wanted, love could be abandoned.

But that's not real love. A particular text in the Hebrew Bible helped me address this issue in my own life. The story of Hananiah, Mishael, and Azariah, better known as Shadrach, Meshach, and Abednego in the Christian tradition, contains an incredible lesson about loving God. As the Babylonian king coerced loyalty and worship to foreign gods from many of the captives, the three Hebrew men refused to submit to the king. Faced with the choice of bowing to the king or being thrown into a fiery furnace, they replied:

> If so it must be, our God whom we serve is able to save us from the burning fiery furnace, and He will save us from your power, O king. But even if He does not, be it known to you, O king, that we will not serve your god or worship the statue of gold that you have set up. (Dan. 3:17–18)

What does love have to do with this, you might ask? In the Hebrew Bible, *hesed* is more than a characteristic of God's relationship to the people; it is a foundation of the covenant concept. Keeping of the faith is never disconnected from love of God. God's offer of the covenant is an act of love; so is the Hebrew people's adherence to that covenant. These three Hebrew men made a choice, and it was more than an act of blind obedience. Rejecting the offer of the Babylonian king was an act of loyalty grounded in *hesed*.

As I have wrestled with the terms of my own love for God, that terse, direct reply to an offer of life in return for misplaced obeisance inspires me. I read it as a sterling example of well-grounded love for the Divine that translates into real, practical choices that affect our lives. Real love is determined, resilient, *hesed*—not based on feelings or the convenience of the moment. Real love is founded on God's unrelenting love of us.

Meister Eckhart offers a brilliant observation about the motivations for love. He writes:

> Whoever dwells in the goodness of God's nature dwells in God's love. Love, however, has no why. If I had a friend and I loved him because of all the good I wished to come to myself through him, I would not love my friend but myself. I ought to love my friend for his own goodness and for his own virtue and for everything that he is in himself.... This is exactly the way it is with people who are in God's love and who do not seek their own interest either in God or in themselves or in things of any kind.... Some people want to love God in the same way as they love a cow. You love it for the milk and the cheese and for your own profit. So do all people who love God for the sake of outward riches or inner consolation. But they do not love God correctly, for they merely love their own advantage.[1]

If we only love God for what we gain from that relationship, we are not loving the Other. We are merely using the relationship for our own gain. That is called exploitation, not love.

But, having recognized the difference between love and exploitation, the act of love may become even more difficult, if for no other reason than we now realize we don't know how to love well! But as we experience divine love in immediate ways, we can learn how to love. One of the best ways to do this is to imitate God's love as we reciprocate it to God with acts of compassion, kindness, and patience.

I cannot overstress, however, that our ability to love God depends absolutely on our first knowing God's love for us. A song we sang in Sunday school when I was a child proclaimed, "Oh, how I love Jesus, because he first loved me." That simple verse is an acknowledgment that our ability to love God is entirely dependent upon having been first loved by the Creator.

Without that primordial love, we scarcely know what pure love is. It is hard to offer what we ourselves do not know or do not have to share. But in the art of thanking and blessing, we have a divine model for real love: it is steadfast (*hesed*), it is a foundational attitude (*ramah*), it is our very essence (*agape*). It teaches us to be passionate about causes that matter. It inspires us to be compassionate, even when we do not have to be. It permits us to be patient when there are a million reasons to lose our cool. We choose to remain grounded, centered, and nonanxious as we wrap our arms around situations, offering a spiritual embrace that cherishes the goodness of creation and the value of the present moment and all who are in it. Once we know this love, new possibilities abound in our ability to practice love out in the world of our everyday lives.

LOVING OTHERS

Just as knowing God's love for us is our greatest resource for healing inner wounds and fears, our love for others is the greatest contribution we make toward healing and transforming a world in desperate search for wholeness. We can enter the world projecting an ambiance of love that can subtly but powerfully alter the way we see and interact with others. In the glow of that ambiance, our commonalities appear more obvious, our differences less divisive. We can imagine a way forward together, collaborating on ideas and projects that are mutually beneficial. The Dalai Lama described it this way:

> If there is love, there is hope that one may have real families, real brotherhood, real equanimity, real peace. If the love within your mind is lost and you see other beings as enemies, then no matter how much knowledge or education or material comfort you have, only suffering and confusion will ensue.[2]

Love may be the remedy, but loving others can be a challenge. Though we are all made in the image of God and have that of God within us, it is also true that we all have rough edges that make us difficult to handle and capable of inflicting pain. In the face of painful challenges, it is instinctual to retaliate or to leave. When others hurt you, particularly those you have committed to love, what is your usual response? Does it flow from love or from self-preservation?

Love can help you find a different tactic. As long as you are not endangered by remaining present, neither retaliate nor flee in the face of pain. Instead, remain calm rather than being swept up in the moment. Look for ways to demonstrate the inherent worth of the other person and love that part of him.

For example, if a friend makes some insensitive remarks out of thoughtlessness or ignorance—or even intentionally because she is upset—you can still choose to respond out of love. First, remember that there is that of God in her, even if she is not acting from that place in the moment. Second, remember that you always have a choice to respond in a deliberate manner, rather than reacting emotionally by shouting or storming off. Third, you can address the issue directly but lovingly, telling your friend why her words were hurtful. This approach may not always be easy, but it does keep the path of blessing open for both of you. By maintaining love, you help make understanding, healing, and reconciliation possible. This is a blessing.

Other times, the source of the problem is closer to home and harder to detect. I think of myself as affable and approachable, but I have had more than one colleague tell me that I can have an intimidating presence. The first time I heard those words, they floored me. I don't know whether it's my size, the volume of my voice, my confidence, or other people's insecurity that creates the sense of intimidation. Whatever its source, those dynamics complicate the relationship in ways that I haven't always been aware of, and those perceptions affect the mood of our interactions. The way of love takes the initiative, however, so these days when I am in a meeting or even greeting people in the hallway, I choose to make an extra effort to create a mood conditioned by the ambiance of love.

Pause for a moment and consider the people you regularly encounter: the mail carrier, the taxi driver, the schoolteacher, the bank teller. Try to imagine how you affect them. Take the initiative to establish a cordial connection. Compliment them. Identify ways you can make their day brighter or more fulfilling.

Some days, loving others is like trying to draw water from an empty well—there seems to be nothing there to give. One of the things I know about myself is that I am an introvert by nature. There comes a point almost every day when I have had all the social interaction I can stand. Unfortunately, the arrival of that point in the day does not always coincide with the end of the day. In those moments, I feel like a caged animal placed in front a crowd. There is no place to hide from their questions and comments. My mind is frustrated. My emotions are edgy. My spirit is uneasy. I feel as though I have nothing to give—especially love—and I fight the urge to lash out at the most innocent of questions and comments. In those moments, love, especially love that imitates the image of God, is a challenge for me—as it may be for you.

It is important to know that even if it feels as though your well is dry, it never really is. In those moments you need strategies for creating brief respites of space and renewal so that divine love can renew your capacity to love. Take a few deep breaths. Steal five minutes behind closed doors. Take a five-minute walk. In each of those moments, remember the source of love that is within you. Because we are made in the divine image and loved from the beginning, this really means that we are incapable of loving until we become aware of the love that has always been ours. Until then, our own spiritual and emotional needs are so demanding that we cannot offer love without ulterior motives. But when we rest in original blessing, we find the trust and confidence in the sufficiency of divine love, which allows us to release the demands we make upon ourselves and others.

But what happens when we disagree strongly, even vehemently? Or when others act inappropriately? Be assured that choosing to project an ambiance of love does not mean that you become a pushover. Love will always seek to speak the truth, because if you wish only the best for the other, you will not create or perpetuate lies and deception. You will, however, learn to speak kindly, *even* in rebuke. Samuel Janney's nineteenth-century history of Quakers provides a useful description of such rebuke:

> About this time John Roberts, of Cirencester, who had formerly been a soldier in Cromwell's army, became a proselyte to the doctrines of Friends, and joined in profession with them. He was very remarkable for his genial humor and ready wit, which rendered his company attractive, and enabled him to administer many an effective, but kindly rebuke to his clerical persecutors. It was remarked of him, by an eminent reviewer, that "every gambling priest and swearing magistrate in the neighborhood stood in fear of his sharp wit."[3]

The identification of Roberts' humor and wit points to a disposition that allowed his commitment to truth and love to be delivered with kindness, even when it involved critical feedback. Indeed, it is much easier to hear such rebuke when it comes from a person we do not fear and whose motives we do not doubt.

We may not all be born comedians, or even prone to much laughter at all. However, I believe that the awareness of love and blessing that comes with this spirituality of gratitude lightens our spirit so that we do not need to be gruff, grumpy, or mean-spirited. There is hardly anything we need to say to one another that cannot be said with civility, if not with humor.

LOVE IS AN ATTITUDE

In the sacred art of thanking and blessing, our love for others begins with an attitude, not a feeling. Given the choice of love, indifference, or hate, we opt for love of our own volition.

A bench under the trees near the Duke University Chapel was the site of an important lesson for me in the power of choice. Judi and I were much involved with one another at the time, but not yet married. One particular day, the fuse of a lingering disagreement caught fire again on a break between classes. Our words were passionate, reaching a point where it is not uncommon for couples to stomp away, or even terminate the relationship. In fact, I thought that is where we were headed. Then, Judi said calmly, "I am in this relationship for the long haul. We are going to have to find a way to resolve this because that is the way love works." Our feelings in that hot moment might have tempted us otherwise, but our intentional decisions set the ground rules. There were no threats. Only commitments. I have never doubted the potential strength and permanence of love since that day.

Pause for a few moments to think about your most important relationships. Are there any where you are allowing an emotional maelstrom to disrupt the love and harmony you desire? Can you see that the strength and love this relationship offers you is much more valuable than the stakes of winning a particular argument? Try saying to the other: "I disagree with you on this, but I value you more than I value winning this argument. Let's try it your way!" Or, "Let's each set aside our agenda and try to imagine a new alternative together."

Love's purest motive is seldom better expressed than when the Buddhist Metta Sutta describes the objectives of loving-kindness: "Let none deceive another … Let him not wish harm to another out of anger or ill will … Let his thoughts of boundless love pervade the whole world."[4] When we see the interconnectedness of all things, our intention is to love every other thing in a manner that seeks happiness and well-being for all and is devoid of self-interest. In particular, the image of our love "pervading the entire world" is worthy of further contemplation. Expressions of ourselves that we send into the public realm have an infinite ripple effect. Anger expressed does not end with the incident in which it erupts. The recipient passes it along, and its effect continues. When we next encounter the person at whom we vented our anger, the effects of that anger will season those future interactions.

Likewise, the effects of love radiate outward and return to us as well. Expressions of love free from the frequent disfigurations we place upon love bounce across the waves of the universe, casting a more wholesome ambiance on the entire picture. At its best, this is blessing exemplified. Life is lived with an absence of malice, but even more, it is lived with the fervent hope of goodwill and happiness for all.

When we are grounded in the basic understanding of blessing as a desire for favor and goodwill, we clearly see the appropriateness of this type of love. Along this path of thanking and blessing, we first learn that we are loved with a cosmic loyalty that cannot be quenched. From the richness of that experience, we commit to imitate that desire for the well-being of all that exists. We wish for their well-being apart from any hope of our own gain. We give out of the generosity of blessing that we receive from the Divine—which proves to be a liberating move. Now our relationships are no longer chess matches in which we need to check the other to assure that we emerge victorious. Our optimistic disposition conditions us to look for the good in the other. We are free to act toward others in ways that contribute constructively to their life's objectives. That is the way of love, without condition.

EXPERIMENTING WITH LOVE

Love always sounds like the perfect solution to many problems, but unless we learn how to offer love it really can't make an impact. We each have three powerful resources at our disposal that help us love effectively, and the path of thanking and blessing draws on them extensively.

The attitude or disposition with which you engage another sends early cues as to the quality of interaction the other can expect from you.

- Harness the energy and insight gained from the Inner Witness and apply it in your interactions with people. Starting with those persons closest to you, commit to interacting positively with them. Act in their best interest without first surveying the potential for personal gain.
- Select one person and choose to love him or her without condition for one week. During that period, compliment him. Build him up whenever the opportunity arises. When he makes a request of you, try to honor it without insisting on anything in return. Refuse to manipulate scenarios to your advantage. When the other person notices the change, tell him why! Try not to be surprised when love begins to make its way back to you.

Speak with an awareness of the power of your words, which is the second resource at your disposal. We can love with our words, but language also injures. From my North Carolina roots, I learned a few phrases that cued me to expect a relational train wreck. They include: "I love her to death, but …"; "With all due respect …"; and "Bless his heart …" Each of these feigns goodwill but generally introduces negative assessments of the other in disrespectful ways. The goal of phrases like these is to undermine and criticize the other, or at least to elevate the speaker. I have seen more than one relationship transformed— for better and for worse—simply by the quality of verbal communication between the two. Verbal messages penetrate to our very core. When we hurt or fear at the core, verbal barbs are like sandpaper on an open wound. Messages of love affirm, empower, and strengthen, serving as a healing balm to the weary soul. Put the resource of your words to work for loving purposes:

- Let your speech flow from the deepest reservoir of love that resides within you by virtue of the Light Within. Let it be filtered by the Inner Witness, who in a moment recognizes your true motives and can offer an accountability checkpoint.
- Monitor the motivation of your speaking.
  - Are you about to speak in order promote or draw attention to yourself?
  - Are the words hurtful, even if true?
  - Can they be restated in ways that allow love to wrap the message's content?
- Commit to bring forth only those responses that desire what is best for the other and offer words in ways that convey that desire.

Any discussion of the practicality of love must come ultimately to the third resource, namely, deeds. More will be said about deeds in other chapters of the book. For now, let us acknowledge that exhortations like those in 1 John 3:18 to love "not in word or speech, but in truth and action" or the Buddhist teaching of *metta* or *ahimsa* sing a common chorus in response to the question of how we love one another. If you really want to be a loving force in this world, pay attention to the deeds you contribute to the cosmic flow.

- Choose actions that do things for others, not to others.
- Learn to labor with those around you in life's difficult moments, rather than work against them.

- Remember that if actions speak louder than words, then love should be more evident in what you do than in what you say.

As you choose the life of thanking and blessing, love is not an obligation to be assumed, but is instead an accurate name for your desire to live as the image of God. Love becomes the guiding principle in your responses to all people, both in word and in deed. As the people in your most immediate circles are touched by this love, their attitudes and activities toward you will transform. In this new ambiance created by the intersection of the Divine Light with your own light, your life's encounters will become a series of thankful and blessed exchanges—not perfect, but never bereft, because the mood is bathed in the greater reservoir of blessed love that keeps you securely within the care of the Divine. Such blessing begets love, which lays the foundation for a differently ordered world.

CREATING A
WELCOMING SPACE

A television news report on the plight of the homeless in the community caught the attention of a friend's young son. His eyes absorbed the haggard images of the men and women interviewed. His five-year-old ears listened to the brief presentations of their life stories. His young mind interpreted the facts. These were real people in his town who had no house of their own, no comfortable room or bed to claim as theirs. Compared with their situations, his family of four lived in a palace, even if it was a modest middle-class dwelling by most standards.

The youngster lobbed questions to his parents, first casually, then with increasing urgency. Why don't they have homes of their own? How did they wind up in this situation? Where are their families? Why is no one helping them? And then it happened. The equation came together in his little mind. "Can we invite them to stay at our house? I can share a room with my sister. They can have my room. We could put blankets on the floor in the living room and more could sleep there."

By then, his sister had joined the chorus. "We have a pantry full of food. We could make Hamburger Helper, or spaghetti for dinner."

The brother piped up—"We have lots of macaroni and cheese they could have. There are six boxes in the pantry." At that point, he lost his sister's support, who drew the line at sharing her mac and cheese.

The documentary sparked an interesting discussion for my friend's family. They did not solve the problem of homelessness. Neither did they invite any of these men and women into their homes, much to their son's chagrin. However, their exchange reminds us that one way to view the world is as a place filled with "haves" and "have nots." The desire to have drives many of us to acquire things we don't really need, and to worry excessively about how to keep what we do have safe and protected. The fear of not having stokes the fires of greed, selfishness, and self-centered perspectives, so that we ignore the needs of others.

Our society often equates blessing with material abundance. If we do not question this assumption, we can easily become ensnared in a mind-set of greed, hoarding, and thoughtless accumulation. The spiritual effect of this mind-set is even more damaging. It repositions us to the center of our worldview. It teaches us to rely only upon ourselves, and to use whatever means are necessary to succeed.

But there is an antidote to this cycle of self-centeredness, and it is a component of the sacred art of thanking and blessing: hospitality. The practice of hospitality challenges our propensity for greed. More than that, the practice of hospitality creates a welcoming space that inspires gratitude and assists in the flow of blessings both offered and received.

HOSPITALITY DESCRIBED

Just what is hospitality? These days, the word tends to connote dinner parties, or else the professional service industry, such as hotels and restaurants. But the central idea of hospitality is an ancient and sacred one, and contains several core components that are important to the art of thanking and blessing.

PROVISION

An episode from the biblical story of Abraham and Sarah demonstrates a traditional and vital component of hospitality— food! As recorded in Genesis 18, Abraham is sitting near the entrance of his tent when guests appear. The sacred context of this encounter is clear, as the guests are variously described as angels, or even God. In any case, when they arrive, Abraham immediately greets them, bows to them, and pleads that he be allowed to offer hospitality in the form of food and drink. They accept, and Abraham and Sarah prepare a feast with the finest ingredients.

Hospitality is imminently practical and is concerned with providing for the guest's physical needs—nourishment, clothing, provisions for the journey. Whatever the guest needs, the host provides. The best hosts will go a step further and try to anticipate a guest's needs so the guest won't feel awkward making a request of the host.

This dynamic is a reflection of our relationship with God. We are sojourners on this earth, just passing through, and just as the Hebrews in the wilderness looked for manna on the ground every morning, so too must we ultimately rely on God to provide for our physical needs. We may till the land, but God makes the crops grow, to paraphrase an old maxim. In this life on earth, we are guests—God's guests. Bearing this in mind helps nurture a sense of gratitude and thankfulness.

In New Testament teachings, Jesus addresses the theme of provision: "Therefore I tell you, do not worry about your life, what you will eat or what you will drink, or about your body, what you will wear. Is not life more than food, and the body more than clothing?" (Matt. 6:25). These words emphasize

God's commitment to provide for our needs; it also prods us to expand our understanding of life's most important matters, for if we are overly concerned with our own needs, we may lose sight of the big-picture questions that affect us all, such as access to health insurance, homelessness, poverty, and global warming. Admittedly, this is easier to believe on a full stomach than on an empty one, but in either case it is an important perspective because it is the basis for our extending hospitality to others. It is part of living in the "image of God"—God demonstrates the spiritual value and importance of hosting, and we, learn to offer hospitality as part of our spiritual practice.

PROTECTION

Another important form of hospitality is offering the guest protection. The story from Genesis 18 picks up on this theme, too. When the men leave Abraham and Sarah, they travel to the city of Sodom, where Abraham's nephew Lot repeats the ritual. It is evening when they arrive, so the offer includes a night's lodging. When people in the town want to mistreat the guests, Lot offers his own daughters to them instead. This sounds horrendous to our ears—an unthinkable decision—but it indicates the seriousness with which a host was charged with his guest's safety. So great is the sacred responsibility that if hardship must be endured, the host would prefer to endure the hardship in order to spare the guests.

As hosts today, we are unlikely to find ourselves in Lot's situation. But what we can take from this story is a question about how practicing hospitality can help us engage with the problems of others. Can we create a welcoming space where they can make their needs known? Will we take the time to listen empathetically to their needs and problems? Sometimes people just need to talk their way through the dilemma at hand. But not always. Can we listen deeply enough to frame possible responses to the issue at hand—even risk a bit of gentle advice? Could we go even further than that, by taking action to help resolve the problem, if we can help? Really extending hospitality means taking an active interest in the problems and welfare of the guest, and working for solutions.

SACRED UNITY

In the flow of life, guests become hosts and later become guests again. Through temporary circumstances (such as going on vacation) or perhaps more drawn-out situations (such as losing a job), we all find ourselves in each of these roles at some point in our lives. This reminds us of the fleeting nature of the circumstances of our lives, but also that none of us is one or the other—rather, we are all connected on a deeper level than it might at first appear.

Even the language of hospitality hints at this. The Indo-European root *ghosti* [1] is the basis for our English words *host* and *hospitality*. Interestingly, it is also the basis for our words *guest* and *stranger*. The fact that these words, which we generally understand to be quite distinct, share a common root is evocative. To offer hospitality is to offer a warm reception to strangers and guests who come to you, but the common root of all four words suggests that there is a more fundamental bond among hosts, guests, and strangers than the roles we play at a given moment. We are all connected in a fundamental way.

It's no surprise, then, that the concept and practice of hospitality has a home in many religious traditions. Hindus call the unexpected guest the *atithi*, literally meaning "without a set time." The Taittiriya Upanishad of the Yajur Veda advises, "Be one to whom the guest is a God."[2] Buddhists refer to *dana*, which consists not so much in the act of giving as in the feeling of wanting to give, of wanting to share what you have with other people. The Jewish mitzvah of *hachnasat orchim* deepens love for God and guests, increasing the joy of all involved. More than mere generosity, altruism, or even social responsibility, these traditions understand the transaction between host and guest to be a sacred one that creates a welcoming space for one another while underscoring our essential unity.

HOSPITALITY EMBRACED

But hospitality is more than a theoretical way to engage the world, and experiencing it deeply leads to profound thankfulness.

I was on the receiving end of hospitality on a trip I took to Central America. During my travels in Guatemala, El Salvador, and Honduras, I stayed in the homes of people who were unknown to me. Our ability to reduce the gulf of mystery between us was limited by my paltry command of Spanish at that time. One family had a room in the courtyard for guests, but not the other two. In one case, a teenage boy stayed with his grandmother for the duration of my visit so that I could have his room. In the other, three adult daughters shared a single room so that I would have a place to sleep.

One day I sat alone on the front porch of the home in Honduras. The front gate was locked for protection, as it always was. Being alone and locked inside, I realized I would have a difficult time leaving if that was what I wanted to do. It occurred to me that I was in a foreign country in a strange neighborhood with no idea of how to get to the airport. I was locked inside a home with people I did not know except that an unknown Quaker, three steps removed from my field of acquaintances, had arranged for my stay. At that point, it became obvious that my trip really was a journey of faith.

A journey of faith, yes, but even more it was an incredible experience of hospitality. One of those daughters came home from school each day to prepare lunch for me. After a night in which I was up several times—quietly, I thought—I found medication for an upset stomach placed by my breakfast plate. When I went for a stroll in the neighborhood, I noticed that the family and their friends always kept a watchful eye on me from a

distance. In the evenings, I was invited to sit with the family and
their friends on the front porch in a gathering that seemed to
have no other purpose than fellowship. A family who did not
know me, but was thrilled that I would journey to their country
simply to build relationships with other Quakers, offered all of
this provision and care. In turn, I was incredibly thankful for
their provision and protection, and I began to see my hosts in a
brand new light.

Hospitality works like that. Generosity allows the guest to
relax and view creation as a friendly place. We can see the world
not as "haves" and "have nots," but as a place of abundance, where
there is plenty of food, plenty of time, plenty of love.

It's worth mentioning that, for those of us who live in rela-
tively safe and prosperous places, it might seem easy to overstate
the effects of hospitality. After all, it's easy to see the world as a
place of abundance if we're well fed and secure. But even when I
was traveling through regions that weren't necessarily safe or
prosperous, people still showed me hospitality. I admired the manner in which the local people chose not to cower behind closed
doors or allow their lives to be ruined by fear. Their love of life
was too great to waste by disengaging from routine activities. For
many of them, their confidence to walk bravely into the marketplace rested on a trust in God that outweighed fear of violence.

The thankfulness we feel from the host's generosity, in turn,
inspires us to find ways to become hosts to those who cross our
paths. The desire to help, already highlighted by the Buddhist
concept of *dana*, is important at this point. Hospitable giving
does not occur out of obligation or coercion, but out of genuine
desire to assist and offer care.

One day I found myself in the middle of a gentle crossfire
between a husband and wife who were friends of mine. The conversation had drifted toward after-dinner routines. The wife
expressed her frustration that she usually bore full responsibility
for doing the dishes. Her husband replied, "I don't mind

helping. All you have to do is ask." Her quick and pointed response was, "That is just it. I don't want to have to ask. I want you to want to help." I have not met many people who "want" to do dishes, but I understand her point. There is a significant difference between acts done out of apathetic willingness and those done out of desire.

The apostle Paul develops this theme in relation to hospitality in his letter to the Corinthians:

> "Each of you must give as you have made up your mind, not reluctantly or under compulsion, for God loves a cheerful giver. And God is able to provide you with every blessing in abundance, so that by always having enough of everything, you may share abundantly in every good work. As it is written, "He scatters abroad, he gives to the poor; his righteousness endures forever." ... You will be enriched in every way for your great generosity, which will produce thanksgiving to God through us; for the rendering of this ministry not only supplies the needs of the saints but also overflows with many thanksgivings to God." (2 Cor. 9:7–12)

Hospitality is first and foremost an act of gratitude to the Creator. Embedded in the culture of hospitality across faith traditions is the expectation that those who are the guest will, at some point, have the opportunity to be the hosts. When the roles are reversed, they will offer the same care and protection to others that they themselves received in their time of need. When we embrace this practice as our own, we offer further evidence that we live and act according to the image of God in which we are made. The responsibility to become hosts to others is, then, a sacred one. We provide for others as the Divine has provided for us. Blessing results from the exchange for both parties—for the guest, because rest and nourishment replenish their strength; for the host, because each act of hospitality teaches them about their own trust and inner resolve to live by faith. In the spiritual realm, the blessings we release return to us multiplied.

The latter point is nicely illustrated in the impressive film *Ushpizin*. It chronicles the life of an impoverished rabbi and his spouse in the days preceding and during the feast of Succoth. In preparation for the feast, the people build temporary dwellings in remembrance of the Hebrew people's journey through the wilderness and to symbolize the transitory nature of life. During the feasts, it is an honor to receive guests. Tradition says they are to be considered as a blessing from God, and that hosts should shower them with hospitality.

In the film, the desired guests arrive in time for the feast, but they are less than honorable men. They disrupt the tranquility of the community and destroy the family's costly citron, a fruit that resembles a lemon. They introduce heartache and doubt into the lives of the characters, who are naturally tempted to expel the guests. Yet they never succumb, but instead maintain their attitude of hospitality. By the end of Succoth, these faithful hosts discover that God has met their deepest needs—the wife is pregnant, money is not scarce, and happiness fills the household again. And the guests recognize that a spiritual transformation is occurring in their own lives as they witness the power of their friends' faith and choose to abandon their dishonorable lifestyle.

The film is a striking example of hospitality as gratitude. By sharing with strangers, we give thanks to God for the provisions with which we have been blessed. The stranger becomes a means by which we offer praise.

HOSPITALITY DEMONSTRATED

Some acts of hospitality are associated with feasts and rituals, and thus have an obviously religious connotation. Other acts of hospitality may appear social or even political in nature, but may still be fundamentally rooted in religious or spiritual conviction.

For example, many Quakers in the nineteenth century worked for the abolition of slavery, and some were actively involved in the Underground Railroad, the network that helped bring escaped slaves to freedom in the North or in Canada. They employed tricks such as secret rooms and wagons with false bottoms to help their "guests" on their journey. Strictly speaking, these were acts of deception, and besides that, were often illegal. And yet, their participation in the Railroad grew explicitly from their religious conviction that owning other human beings was wrong. They provided provision and protection, and they viewed the escaped slaves as fellow human beings, not as property. This was a form of hospitality.

A less politically charged remnant of that practice is the *Directory for Traveling Friends*. This book provides names and addresses of Friends worldwide who are willing to offer hospitality to traveling Friends who have a letter of introduction from their Monthly Meeting. This is no small act, as participating Friends are willing to open their homes to strangers whose only means of credibility is that other Friends have recommended them.

As we travel the path of thanking and blessing, our Inner Witness nudges us to take yet another courageous step forward toward our own fulfillment and our standing invitation to participate with God in the ongoing creation of a more loving world. Stepping forward to offer hospitality to friends, guests, and strangers, we stand at the threshold of a different engagement with the universe. We have increased confidence in the possibility to encounter the Divine in all times and places. We hold an optimistic disposition toward the universe we inhabit. We have decided to make love the foundation of our interactions. As we live with these changes, hospitality calls us out. In response, we answer its summons to offer more than sweet disposition or theoretical constructs about how the world should operate.

How do we answer in a way that offers spiritual hospitality? At the end of the day, spirituality is nothing more than "lived faith." We embody our spiritual convictions, whether in the faithful observance of ritual that is meaningful to us or in more mundane acts that fill our daily schedules. Hospitable acts express the inner convictions and dispositions developed in the art of thanking and blessing. Concrete acts that we give to those who travel our way are demonstrations of our own gratitude for God's provision to us. As we offer nourishment to others— whether it is lodging for the night, a cup of cold water, a ride to the supermarket, or a listening ear—we support them on the journey they must travel. As we give them hospitality, we encourage—even prepare—them to bless others according to what they have received. In turn, we are blessed by the knowledge that we have shaped a holy moment—that of God in us reached out to that of God in the other—and been part of the positive transformation of one small speck of time.

STEPPING BEYOND FEAR

Stories like Abraham's invitation to the visitors, or the narrative in Luke 9 where Jesus miraculously multiplies five loaves of bread and two fish to feed five thousand people, teach us lessons far beyond merely opening our homes to others or serving physical nourishment to the hungry. Hospitality is much more than that—it is an attitude of embrace, a bear hug for the universe. This is no small matter. Think for a moment of many of the messages that bombard us daily. Commercials teach us to fear that our identities will be stolen and our credit scores ruined. Stories of theft, murder, and violence dominate local news. World politics elevate the fear of cultural, national, and religious differences. There is some truth to each of those warnings, but when taken as the sole source of information on which we base our strategies for engaging the world they drive divisive wedges of fear and suspicion between strangers and ourselves.

For example, in the rural setting where I was raised, there was a strong, unwritten rule that we distrusted "city-folk," Northerners, and fast-talking salespersons who showed up at our door with the latest novelty we supposedly shouldn't live without. The value of the known network, or at least trustworthy connections, was the difference between immediate acceptance and infinite relational purgatory.

Safety and reasonable suspicion are always in order, but we should not adopt a default point of view that everything unknown is to be distrusted or feared. A commitment to hospitality counters that deceptive viewpoint. It views the stranger as a guest, not a foreigner. It recognizes the guest as one sent by the Divine. It understands that the encounter blesses the host as well as the guest. It interprets occasions of need as opportunities to trust and assist, rather than as moments to tighten our grip on what we have. It welcomes rather than locks out.

Choosing hospitality is another liberating moment in the spiritual journey. Trusting in God, we learn that the burdens of the entire world do not rest upon our shoulders. We are not responsible for solving every existing problem; we are merely asked to share according to what we have received with those people who intersect our path. Acts of hospitality uplift our spirits as we discover we can make tangible differences in the lives of others. Our confidence increases as our generosity is received with gratitude that sends signals of affirmation and value in response to our embrace.

EXPERIMENTING WITH HOSPITALITY

You have the opportunity to make your corner of the world a more welcoming, hospitable place. How might you begin to experiment with this gift?

Consider whether you have a gift for hospitality that would allow you to provide overnight accommodations or meals to guests for a temporary period.

- Start with organizations to which you already belong. If they bring guests to town, perhaps you can offer hospitality to them. For some travelers, the warmth of a home is preferable to the isolation of a hotel room.
- Think about the things that make for a relaxing, comfortable stay when you are in a strange place: cool refreshment upon arrival, plush towels for the bath, inviting conversation… Go the extra mile to attend to these small details.

A senior-citizen friend of mine tells me "folks do not know how to 'neighbor' the way they used to." Societal mobility and relocation, busy schedules, and distrust of the unknown all contribute to this weak connection. Many of us have little more than a "pass and wave" relationship with the people on our block.

- Consider hosting a neighborhood dinner. There is no need to feel responsible for providing all the food if that is too burdensome. Leading the initiative and establishing the hospitable context for the gathering would be an incredible boost to an idea like this. In doing so, you will open doors for communication and the building of a wider network of familiarity.

Not all hospitality requires offering lodging and food in your physical space!

- Practice hospitality over the phone. This begins with good phone etiquette, but does not end there. The tone of voice and the manner in which you receive a call can offer hospitality. I confess to a deep dislike of telemarketing phone calls. Even so, I have determined to be kind and hospitable as I decline their offers. When there is a real person on the other end of that phone, then I am speaking with someone created in the image of God. This is someone of value. This person has a life—perhaps family—with hopes, dreams, and financial needs. For whatever reason, this is the venue by which they earn a living. They deserve a hospitable world just as I do; I can say "no" respectfully and politely.

There are many other simple ways you can offer hospitality in the form of a symbolic embrace that provides encouragement for others on their journey.

- Choose not to be first in line at the bank or the grocer. Let the person in an obvious hurry have the taxi or the older person have the remaining seat on the bus.
- Spend a day doing what your family prefers to do instead of the things you planned to do.
- On a more global scale, refrain from material excess. The fact that you can afford multiple homes, automobiles, or pairs of shoes does not mean you should buy them. By not purchasing, you lessen demand and increase supply, making it possible for others to find their place at the table. In short, recognize the abundance and satisfaction that is yours, and make room for someone else to find fulfillment.

As you live in ways that undermine tendencies toward greed and fear, you will experience the immediate benefit of a more relaxed, confident demeanor. As you embrace guests and invite them into your domain in appropriate ways, those new acquaintances enrich your life because every personality has something to contribute to your pleasure and knowledge of the world. That is an immediate experience of blessing to the host, even as the host's provision blesses the guest. As your hospitality creates a more blessed universe, that blessing comes back to you when you become a guest or stranger instead of a host. For as you sow, you also reap. The seeds of hospitality planted now bring you a harvest of blessing when you are in need.

HOPE SPRINGS INTERNAL

M y father-in-law is a retired United Methodist minister. One of his first appointments was to a little church in the southern Indiana town of Fairfield. It was a small town, sporting a general store, an elementary school, and of course, a post office—nothing solidifies a town's right to exist more than a zip code. It was not an extraordinary town, but then most places aren't. Extraordinary or not, it was home to its residents and that was enough to elicit their fierce loyalty. The town anchored their ordered world, contributing to their sense of identity and understanding of community, all of which came under threat.

The Army Corps of Engineers was building dams and creating reservoirs at strategic locations in an effort to control flooding along the Ohio River during the 1950s and 1960s. They were considering the Fairfield, Indiana, area as a possible location for managing the flow of the Whitewater River, which empties into the Ohio. Government officials made extended presentations locally about issues related to the dam. Of course, local residents opposed it and continued the debate anywhere they happened to gather—church parking lots, school auditoriums, the supermarket, and so on. In time, the powers that be decided to build the dam. The entire area, including the little town of Fairfield, would then be underwater. Authorities made plans to relocate residents, schools, and even cemeteries.

Until the decision was final, hope fueled the determined efforts of those who opposed the building of the dam. My father-in-law remembers that once the decision was finalized, however, everything changed. People stopped mowing their lawns and trimming their hedges. House repairs ceased, lending a dilapidated look and feel to the neighborhood. Trash began to pile up along the streets. Once the last wisp of hope evaporated, the town residents saw no need to exercise further care and responsibility. They lost energy and direction because they saw no new possibilities for the future. They just gave up.

Hope inspires and motivates. It gives us a vision for an improved future. In the path of thanking and blessing, this is not blind optimism. Rather, it is founded on our experience that we are rooted in original blessing. Other practices, such as hospitality, reinforce the fundamental benevolence of the universe and our role in it. Our dreams matter, and they aren't unattainable fantasies. We can make a difference in making them come about. This is the birth of hope. In time, our words and actions based in hope can even become prophetic levers for change, not just in our own lives, but in entire systems. All of this introduces more blessing into the world.

THE THINGS WE HOPE FOR

Hope is all about possibilities. In its most basic sense, hope is an emotional state that expresses our deep desire for a particular outcome in a given situation, such as the birth of a healthy child, a promotion at work, or world peace. More than merely a desire, hope is wrapped up in the possibility that the desire can be realized—that what is lacking can be fulfilled, or that injustices can be put right. To the external observer, another person's hope may look like blind optimism or even absolute foolishness. That assessment generally will not discourage the person maintaining the hope, who feels completely justified in holding the position.

An extreme example might be the prisoner-of-war, whose isolation, mistreatment, and bleak future provide ample reason to despair or even quit. Yet, most of us have heard those incredible stories of hope—buoyed by a faded photo of a loved one or by old-fashioned grit—in which someone's will to live sustains him until his release or rescue. As the Fairfield residents demonstrated, as long as hope is present we are capable of believing and acting with determination and purpose, whatever the odds against us. Our desires may not come to pass, but we are not defeated unless we ourselves give up hope.

Religious conviction often plays a powerful role in shaping hope. The reasons for this are simple, really. Religions offer particular worldviews of how a rightly ordered world operates. These visions inspire us. It may be the vision of a perfect state of consciousness, such as the Buddhist nirvana, a more concretely (if metaphorically) envisioned kingdom of God where the lion will lie down with the lamb, or the restoration of the right order, long since lost, as with the Hebrew prophets:

> In the days to come,
> The Mount of the Lord's House shall stand
> Firm above the mountains;
> And it shall tower above the hills.
> The peoples shall gaze on it with joy,
> And the many nations shall go and shall say:
> "Come,
> Let us go up to the Mount of the Lord,
> To the House of the God of Jacob;
> That He may instruct us in His ways,
> And that we may walk in His paths."

> For instruction shall come forth from Zion,
> The word of the Lord from Jerusalem. (Mic. 4:1–2)

Whatever the specific content, these visions can become our goal and orient our actions in life. When we decide to work toward those visions, we become transformed, and we help transform and bring blessings to the world around us.

WHEN HOPE IS FRUSTRATED

Hope empowers us to work toward our vision, but it is no guarantee that we will succeed. In fact, our unrealized dreams and disappointments can build up like a reservoir of frustration and resentment. This may be expressed subtly, such as when I hear a middle-aged parent remember the dreams of her youth—"I wanted to be a nurse"—that were placed on hold in favor of other options that seemed appropriate at the time, but appear less so now. Or these frustrations might build and build until the dam gives way in an explosion of an emotional breakdown. In any case, no one lives an ideal life with all her dreams and hopes realized.

One reason we sometimes don't reach our dreams is that those we work with don't share the dreams. I deal with this on a professional level. My primary work at this point in my life is providing leadership within a small faith tradition that has more baggage than a secondhand luggage store. I have a vision for how my tradition can be more vital—practically relevant in the lives of its members, and meaningfully engaged in creating a healthier, more hopeful world—and I have hope that we can actually achieve that goal. Yet, Quakerism's strong antihierarchical and antiauthoritarian roots leave us suspicious of leadership, and this undermines progress. I have now been serving Friends in some capacity for twenty-five years, and I've never been so frustrated! Some days I believe that some people in my tradition simply don't believe we can, or need to, address our chronic weaknesses and envision a stronger future. They have no hope.

Recently, I said to a friend, "I don't mind playing for an under-dog, but the team needs to want to win." These spontaneous words resonated deeply within me when they first sneaked out. What I believe it means is that I know I have a limited time to work in this life. I would prefer not to spend it, even waste it, for a cause where people have lost hope and, with it, their fighting spirit. I concur with Dante, who wrote long ago in *Divine Comedy*, "Life without hope is hell." If it is not in your starting lineup, what's the point of getting in the game at all?

Another reason our goals are sometimes not realized is that we have different, even conflicting, hopes. Our particular dreams and aspirations motivate us, and make perfect sense to us. Oddly enough, our ideals are not always in accord with the ideals others may hold. It's been said that wherever three people come together for discussion, there will be four opinions because someone will be of two minds on the subject. We catch a glimpse of hope's complexity when we recognize that as we each work toward our goals, we may at times innocently work against each other. We strive toward our different ideals within limited space and resources that we share with everyone else, and not everyone can win. Different goals, different strategies, and shared resources on the common playing field of life complicate our achievement of hopes and aspirations. Some hopes will never be realized.

"Hoping" Mechanisms

What happens when our hopes are not realized? Typically, we use one or more coping mechanisms to try to maintain our opti-mism. Each of these can be helpful in its own way, but as we shall see, the path of thanking and blessing offers an alternative and a deeper understanding of hope.

One way we cope with disappointment, especially if we are religious, is to remember the tenets of our faith as a foundation and justification for our hope. Consider the sentiment of the Christian tradition, particularly in light of a delay in the anticipated return of Jesus: "Now faith is the assurance of things hoped for, the conviction of things not seen" (Heb. 11:1) or "For in hope we were saved. Now hope that is seen is not hope. For who hopes for what is seen? But if we hope for what we do not see, we wait for it with patience" (Rom. 8:24–25). Here, faith underpins hope and negates the power of unfulfilled expectations. It inspires continued trust that God, and the ideals associated with God, will prevail at a later time. It encourages believers to remain steady in their devotion until the day when their hopes about the kingdom of God are fulfilled. The details of hope vary across religions traditions, but they share a common feature—faith sustains it.

The degree of frustration and suffering we can endure with the power of faith is nothing short of incredible. I knew a woman, now deceased, whose hope left me speechless. She spent her early years in a mental hospital, until doctors discovered she was epileptic rather than mentally ill. She was an adult before she was released. Once released, she managed to purchase a small home of her own but really had no means to sustain herself other than with government aid. She lived on the "wrong side of town" and was ridiculed by many local residents. She told me she was actually unwelcome in some churches in her town. She sang like an Appalachian angel and cussed like a seasoned sailor, often in the same breath.

When I asked her how she survived when so many people seemed to be against her, she shared her hope with me. She believed deeply—all the way down to the marrow in her bones—that God was her constant companion and her source of strength, so she lived accordingly. Though some people in the medical field thought she could not live alone, she refused to accept their conclusion. When neighbors shunned her because she kept to herself, she never missed an opportunity to offer a kind deed to them when she could. And she was fortunate to find a few people who, like her, were mildly ostracized, and they became her circle of friends. I never understood how any of this was financially feasible, but she always seemed to have what she needed. Her hope was simple, adamant, and unquestioning, grounded in her faith that God had never abandoned her and would always provide for her needs.

Another way some people manage unfulfilled expectations is with an unwavering insistence that God will provide some other way in the future. The current sufferings are insignificant because greater rewards lie in the future—if not in this world, then in the next one. The fact that you did not receive a particular job is acceptable because it means God has something better in store for you. Hope lessens the impact of tragedy or death if it allows the expectation of reunion in the next life. Martyrdom is an honor when hope promises rewards in the afterlife.

Another method of dealing with frustration is to remember our finitude and our very limited perspective of the whole. Faced with inexplicable scenarios and hardships, we comfort ourselves with the belief that God knows all things, and that there is a hidden purpose that we are yet to understand. I encountered an upset woman in a supermarket one day who quietly muttered a simple refrain throughout the store: "They meant it for my bad, but God meant it for my good." Drawing from the Joseph story in Genesis, this refrain appeals to God's knowledge and awareness that towers above our ability to know how things will ultimately work for our good. Whatever inexplicably bad things had happened to her, she comforted herself by knowing that God knew the whole story.

Sometimes we minimize our disappointments by reframing our expectations. If in midlife we discover that we never reached the goals of our youth, we maintain hope of a fulfilled life if we convince ourselves that the original goals would not have made us happy, but our current ones are bringing fulfillment.

Some forms of religious belief offer more stringent responses to the frustration of unfulfilled expectations, including apocalyptic literature, which comforts the reader by staking its hopes on an outside deliverer who will come in some remote (or sometimes imminent) future. Other forms refer to the distant past and the mysterious power associated with creation, encouraging us to transcend suffering and disappointment and to understand that life's fullest meaning is found in a relationship with the Creator.

Each of these strategies has a moment in the sun and is helpful from time to time, but none is an ultimate solution. The art of thanking and blessing leads us to a different place.

A LIVING HOPE

Thanking and blessing helps us focus on the experience of the moment and the optimism and gratitude that arises from the blessings we have already received. This gives rise to a different kind of hope, one that motivates us to act, but that also keeps us centered in all the possibilities inherent in the now. Instead of locking us into a single vision of the future, a living hope helps us be more flexible. We still have vision, but it serves to orient us in the direction that we, and possibly all of creation, should be moving. We become less concerned that the actual result match the final expectations we carry in our own heads. This kind of hope is adaptable to changing situations, without our having to resort to the coping mechanisms described above.

Hope sustained by a spirituality of thanking and blessing is a living hope. The early Quaker Isaac Penington expressed the essence of such hope nicely in "Ways of Life and Death Made Manifest":

> There springs up an [sic] hope, a living hope, in the living principle, which hath manifested itself, and begun to work. For the soul truly turning to the light, the everlasting arm, the living power is felt; and the anchor being felt, it stays the soul in all the troubles, storms, and tempests it meets with afterwards....[1]

It is a living hope that we seek—one resulting from the power of a dynamic relationship with the Divine that anchors our very being. We seek a hope that rests upon the certainty of the inner dialogue we have with God in the Inner Sanctuary of our soul. We desire a hope that materializes from the new awareness we have achieved regarding our relationships with God, ourselves, and the world through these spiritual practices associated with thanking and blessing.

The thankfulness of that experience means that hope springs internal. We discover this is a formidable hope, not easily crushed—an experience that only intensifies when we learn the art of sacramental living. We don't look for outside deliverance, and we don't lower our expectations. Instead, we remain steadfastly optimistic about the possibility of change in any situation, beginning with ourselves. Life is our playground, not our battlefield; God is our constant companion, not an absentee landlord. This is the reason for our cheerful disposition. We are not blind to the pain and brokenness of our world, but our experience of God and the boundless possibilities that lie within us and among us create a groundswell of hope as we are attuned to the Divine Presence.

For example, we can hope for a world where everyone awakens to the reality of divine blessing surrounding and indwelling us—without expecting people to "convert" to our point of view. We can envision an alternative to religious and political ideologies that choose to dominate and subjugate others simply because we do not understand those differences—without trying to enforce such an agenda on those we know. We can imagine leaving the task of judging another's worth to some jury other than our own, freeing us to focus on the ways we bless and fortify persons we love and activities in which we are involved. We long for a society fashioned with networks of spiritual intimacy, mutual respect, and commitment to the common good.

When love and hospitality are the natural expressions of faithful living, we can expect that a hope such as this is possible. Love and hospitality create a sense of support and safety; they also nurture attitudes of trust and abundance. Settings like these create an ethos in which we easily practice mutual encouragement. An attitude of hope is nurtured, partly because we enjoy such a trusting relationship with the Divine, partly because we have appropriate confidence in ourselves, and partly because we experience a friendly universe in which the possible is imaginable, and the imaginable takes on a degree of probability.

Once we choose this as our spiritual path, the practice of thanking and blessing will supplant old assumptions that life cannot get better, that change is unlikely, and that individuals are helpless victims of the resulting chaos. This defeatist mentality is at odds with a spirituality that embraces the possibilities of transformation. When I was a young adult searching for a relevant and practical faith, words from the New Testament Book of Ephesians resonated deeply with me:

> I pray that, according to the riches of his [God's] glory, he may grant that you may be strengthened in your inner being with power through his Spirit, and that Christ may dwell in your hearts through faith, as you are being rooted and grounded in love. I pray that you may have the power to comprehend, with all the saints, what is the breadth and length and height and depth, and to know the love of Christ that surpasses knowledge, so that you may be filled with all the fullness of God. Now to him who by the power at work within us is able to accomplish abundantly far more than all we can ask or imagine...."
> (Eph. 3:16–20)

Quakers like me eschew creeds, but if I were to ever have one, this would be a contender for the prize. It acknowledges God's care for humanity. It understands the inner life where the spirit of God dwells. It focuses on love as a response to this experience. And last but not least, it embraces the power of possibility, which is hope.

A PROPHETIC EDGE

With time we will find that our lives, while uplifting others, will also offer a bit of a prophetic edge. We may lack the polish and universal flair that Micah's vision introduced earlier, but we will be no less prophetic. As our hope innocently infiltrates the circles in which we travel, we will elevate the standards of expectation for others as well as ourselves. When we encounter dismay or despair, our worldview will interject a different perspective. When we witness repeated injustice or apathy, we may well ask others if we can collectively imagine a new possibility. To a greater and greater degree, our hopes are focused on our ability to participate in God's creative work rather than in waiting for God to conform the world to relieve our frustrations. This can begin in the smallest of acts that inspire confidence in the goodness of humanity and hope for a just world.

I experienced such a moment while traveling in Denmark a few years ago. I sat with three family members on a bench inside an amusement park enjoying an ice cream cone after dinner one evening. A young man approached me, and I instinctively suspected he would ask me for money. I wanted to avoid contact with him. When our eyes met he extended his hand, and I prepared to recoil, but his question surprised me. "Excuse me, sir," he said. "Are these yours?" In his hand he held my driver's license, credit card, and health insurance card, all of which had fallen out of my wallet while I paid for the ice cream. The bad news in the story is that apparently I do resemble the photo on my driver's license. In the plus column, though, was my sense of gratitude at the honesty of this stranger who took the time to identify me in a crowd and return my articles. Mingled with the gratitude was a slight internal reprimand for my ungrounded suspicion.

You and I can inspire that kind of hope for a just and friendly world. I have paid for the repair of an automobile trans- mission for a family trying to make it across the country, bought a bus ticket for a man newly released from prison to give him a new start on his dreams, and even walked a lost, naked five- year-old through a strange neighborhood until he was finally able to identify his house. What are some of the small kindnesses you have done for others that made you feel like an agent of hope? If all you ever do on behalf of hope is share good acts with an unsuspecting public, you will bless the world in ines- timable ways.

EXPERIMENTING WITH HOPE

One of the simplest and most direct ways of spreading hope has been well illustrated in the film *Pay It Forward*. The plot built upon the idea of doing good deeds for others with no expectation of being rewarded. As a person received a kind act or a helping hand, the recipient was asked only to "pay it forward," or pass it along to someone else. I think it is one of the simplest ways to begin partic- ipating in this spiritual practice. One wrinkle in the plan is that it requires continued commitment. Otherwise, it will be yet another good idea that ran out of steam, much to our collective regret.

- Help create a more hopeful world by "paying it for- ward" at least two times each day. Build a pattern of practice that will soon become a personal habit.
- If you are eager to try more, create a context in which you offer grace, compassion, and encouragement and you will have the privilege of watching a life bloom before your eyes as you enrich it with your blessing, and almost inevitably, the other person will rise to this stan- dard in his or her treatment of you.

- Exercise gentle leadership in the circles where you operate, be it the workplace, with peer groups, or in volunteer scenarios. Many decisions are made based on fear, greed, or suspicion, and these breed a sense of hopelessness. Imagine the value of your interjecting a different point of view into discussions mired in those destructive ruts.

  - Offer pointed, but positively stated, counterpoints when you sense that poor decisions are about to be made.
  - Ask questions that allow others to explain why they are drawn to one solution or another. Be sure to articulate your own reasons for thinking differently on a matter.
  - As you discover people willing to try new ideas, create an atmosphere where others feel free to express themselves and risk new things. One of the messages I repeatedly tell members of my office staff is that I do not care how many mistakes they make unless they are making the same mistakes repeatedly.

When hope is a motivating force within us, we choose a life that invigorates rather than hibernates. We look to engage, rather than withdraw. We seek to confidently explore our surroundings and share our blessings. If you have come this far down the path of thanking and blessing, you know by now that under a bushel is no place to put a candle. Your own light has intensified, and light cannot help but illuminate. This is not an illumination of haughtiness or self-righteousness, but of strong love and honest compassion.

Hopeful people are catalysts. If you come bearing hope, you introduce the possibility for change. When people are immersed in a situation, it can be difficult to see things with fresh eyes. A new idea or perspective could catch on easily and be all that is needed to transform a discouraging situation. At that point, you have not only succeeded in spreading hope, but you have also helped unleash new creative energy into the universe. Your life will be one that speaks volumes, even without lots of words— more on that in the next chapter.

LIVES THAT SPEAK LOUDER THAN WORDS

"Let your word be 'Yes, Yes' or 'No, No'; anything more than this comes from the evil one" (Matt. 5:37). This teaching of Jesus is music to the ears of a person of few words, but its power extends beyond its delightful message to introverts. More than a maxim for truthfulness, this aphorism calls for consistency between our words and deeds. The Talmud teaches that the first question asked at the Throne of Judgment is not about belief or ritual, but "Have you dealt honorably, faithfully in all your dealings with your fellowman?" (Talmud, *Shabbat* 31a). Each of these teachings is a call for personal integrity—a quality that resonates with the sacred art of thanking and blessing.

We make hundreds of decisions in any given day. The decision making starts early in the morning with boring choices of what to wear. As we drive along the highway, we make split-second assessments about running a yellow light. At work, we make other judgments, such as how to construct a sales presentation from which we will personally profit if successful. In all those decisions, we choose how to represent ourselves to others.

We can choose to obey traffic signals or throw caution to the wind. We can make an honest, realistic sales pitch, or we can make false claims for the sake of the sale. We can be completely honest in our interactions with others, or take a more guarded approach in sharing what is on our minds. Moments of self-presentation are opportunities to decide whether we will speak and act with integrity or not. These are not only decisions about *what we do*, but they are also decisions about *how we will be*. For example, suppose a cashier gives you an extra five dollars when she returns your change. If you have already decided that you *are* an honest person, then there is no question of whether or not you will point out the error and return the five dollars. In returning the money, you demonstrate that there is a consistency between what you desire to be and how you actually conduct yourself.

We can commit to integrity in our actions and words, and give honest, accurate information to the world. But what about the information we receive from others? Can it always be trusted? We send vital information to others, and we depend on the information they send to us. Whether we are giving or receiving information in any particular moment, we are participating in a grand universe of interconnectedness and interdependency. The quality of the information we offer to each other influences our respective abilities to make sound decisions. Integrity matters. It makes reliability, trust, and confidence possible—each of which enhances our gratitude and perpetuates our commitment to bless others.

The presence or absence of trust has an impact on our lifestyles. Imagine the effect on our quality of life, even our psyches, when relationships are little more than a house of cards built on lies and untrustworthy information. Isn't it unsettling to worry that strangers who approach you, whether on the street, on the Internet, or by phone, have ulterior motives and may choose to deceive you?

But what if things were different? What if you knew that every time you asked questions, you were certain to receive honest, reliable answers? Can you imagine the confident, even thankful, feeling that would accompany your every move if you could count on everyone you interacted with to be trustworthy? Would you be able to give, share, and bless more freely in such a user-friendly environment?

When we can trust the integrity of others' actions, motives, and words, then we can spend less time and energy in a defensive mode, protecting ourselves against deception and manipulation. In the secure environment integrity and trust afford us, we can more easily share the richness of our gratitude and blessing as we interact with others. Integrity allows us to live "at face value"—what we see is what we get, and what we get is the best we have to offer one another. No strings. No tricks. No gimmicks. As we practice the sacred art of thanking and blessing, we cast our web of influence as wide as possible. Working together in that way, we collectively raise the quality of our interactions and relationships.

INTEGRITY DESCRIBED

A call for integrity is a call for consistency between beliefs and actions, between words and deeds. Integrity gives evidence— evidence that our lives demonstrate the convictions, commitments, and loyalties we claim to embrace. From a faith perspective, integrity shows congruence between the lives we live and the values and expectations we adopt in our spiritual journey—whether we identify with a particular tradition or not.

For example, if the teachings of your tradition describe God as holy and you accept that as true, then a life of integrity means you will want to know how to relate to a holy God, and then live accordingly—perhaps incorporating certain rituals, times of prayer, or manners of dress into your daily routines. If your tradition understands the goal of life as one in which your greatest purpose is to overcome ignorance, then integrity would require that your life be ordered in ways that help you overcome it. If your life's greatest goal is to love others, then integrity requires that you learn how your tradition shows love—perhaps through kind acts or feeding the hungry or working for justice—and then live a life that loves well.

Questions about integrity are especially pertinent when you consider how you are to live alongside others who are different from you. If your tradition excludes those who do not adopt the beliefs you hold, then integrity will require that you separate from them or convert them. If your tradition respects other faith traditions, then you can learn to live alongside others in mutually respectful ways without compromising your integrity.

For some groups, achieving integrity involves maintaining the group's particular belief system without breach or compromise. Conservative Christian standards safeguarding the people's holiness and sanctification, Zionist Jewish teachings preserving identity and faith from external influence, and Islamic guidance to restore and preserve the *fitrah*, or innate purity, are examples of this approach to integrity. For less doctrinaire traditions, integrity hinges upon holding right beliefs and following them for the purpose of achieving a particular state of being, as with the Buddhist eight elements of *sammā*, which outline a holistic understanding of integrity as a means of achieving enlightenment. Within the Quaker tradition, integrity is held as an important testimony, or outward expression, of faith; as a noncreedal tradition, Quakerism maintains that standards for integrity are to be discerned from our experience of the Light Within, held in tension with feedback from our faith community.

But how can so many different, and seemingly contradictory, religious teachings all lead down the path of integrity? It's a question of individual consciousness. As you engage your Inner Witness, what do you make of your encounters with the Divine? How do you perceive God, think about yourself, and engage the world? What attitudes, practices, or actions would be appropriate responses to the conclusions you are drawing from your encounters with the Divine?

That is the issue at the heart of discussions about standards of faith and living with integrity according to those standards. Every religion has such standards, though they may differ from tradition to tradition. Indeed, not everyone within a single tradition can agree on the specifics. But this can be valuable, in fact, because holding various views in tension can be a catalyst calling us to a greater, more intentional integrity. Inspect any tradition you want, and you will likely find a lively history of debate about how one lives with faithful integrity.

I love the spirit of this debate that is captured in the pages of the Hebrew Bible. On the one hand, the covenant given to the people through Moses in the Book of Exodus as the Hebrews journeyed toward the Promised Land details broad standards for community life. These standards are developed further in later chapters of Exodus, Leviticus, and Deuteronomy. To hear the prophets describe things, there were moments when the priests and people focused too much attention on details and rituals—to the point that religious practice became detached from the spirit of the covenant. In light of that, the prophets decried a lack of consistency among covenantal values, love of God, and social interactions. The prophet Micah gives a superb example of this when he exclaims that all God really desires is for people to act justly, love mercy, and walk humbly with their God (Mic. 6:8).

As we contemplate the subject of integrity in this chapter, I am not advocating for a particular code. Instead, I am speaking of a desired consistency between our values, whatever they may be, and our actions, rather than elevating a particular code of ethics for adoption. The sacred art of thanking and blessing is spirituality grounded in a *way to be*. This manner of being embraces an understanding of an immanent God and encourages cultivating an awareness of the Divine Presence. It celebrates cheerful, thankful engagement with creation, with expectations of being blessed from that interaction. Love and hospitality are identified, in broad strokes, as extremely useful ways of expressing our thankfulness and contributing blessing to the world. Like painting on a canvas, those broad strokes will be filled in with myriad details as we decide what to interject and how to respond day by day.

INTEGRITY MODELED

A story that is perhaps apocryphal circulates in Quaker circles and involves William Penn, who was a first-generation Quaker. He was born into the English aristocracy, but came to America to establish a colony—Pennsylvania—founded upon Quaker principles. Early in their development, Quakers adopted a peace testimony as part of their faithful witness. They disavowed all war, claiming that Christ eliminated the occasion of war.

It is said that when Penn first became convinced of Friends' principles, he did not immediately relinquish his sword, as it was customary for men of rank and fashion to wear one. One day he asked George Fox for his advice on the matter. Fox's reply was that Penn should wear the sword as long as he was able to do so—meaning that until such time as Penn felt inwardly convinced to lay it aside, he was not expected to do so. A short time later, Fox again saw Penn and observed that he was no longer wearing his sword. Penn responded that he had taken Fox's advice, and that he was no longer able to wear the sword in good conscience. The point of the anecdote is that individuals should be led by the promptings of the Divine, and that this, rather than the opinions of others, sets the standard of integrity.[1]

In the sacred art of thanking and blessing, the look and feel of personal integrity results from your alignment of self with the Spirit of the Divine that indwells you. It is the product of your Inner Witness urging the manifestation of this new perspective on your outward interactions and transactions. The teachings and guidelines of your chosen tradition, if any, can help, but ultimately living with integrity calls for reflective engagement with the Holy rather than adherence to a set code.

As you continue down the path of thanking and blessing, you continually undertake intentional reflection on your experience of God. These experiences instill new insights into your consciousness. They open your eyes to new perspectives. As you see the world through freshly opened eyes, your opinions and values will likely change. You cannot know whether you are living a life of integrity until you can name the things that matter most to you. With that in mind, take a walk or find a quiet place and mull over this question: when you imagine your most passionate dream for your life—the scenario you believe would bring you the most peace, happiness, and satisfaction—who and what emerges as most important to you? Does the current ordering of your life reflect their importance?

Quakers are fond of saying that a person should "mind the measure of Light that has been given." This is an acknowledgment that we are all on a journey of discovery. Faith is a process, as is our own transformation. What a relief to realize that we are not responsible for meeting some highly set, impossible standard of perfection. Instead, we are only responsible for living—that is to say, embodying or manifesting—those things we have learned to date. This is integral in a discussion about integrity. If you adopt this perspective as your own, introspection and self-reflection become natural precursors to integrity.

To assist with this type of introspection, Quakers have long used a device known as "queries" that proves quite useful. They are sometimes read in gatherings for worship or in private devotions. These are probing questions that, when thoughtfully engaged, can lead us to decisions grounded in integrity of purpose. As examples, here are two queries from Britain Yearly Meeting's *Quaker Faith and Practice*:[2]

Are you honest and truthful in all you say and do? Do you maintain strict integrity in business transactions and in your dealings with individuals and organisations? Do you use money and information entrusted to you with discretion and responsibility? Taking oaths implies a double standard of truth; in choosing to affirm instead, be aware of the claim to integrity that you are making.

If pressure is brought upon you to lower your standard of integrity, are you prepared to resist it? Our responsibilities to God and our neighbour may involve us in taking unpopular stands. Do not let the desire to be sociable, or the fear of seeming peculiar, determine your decisions.

When I was a child, I thought queries were the path of least resistance for the spiritually inclined. I was not expected to recite a particular set of answers. I could answer "no" to any question I did not like and move on with my day. The ignorant bliss of my youth has passed, and I now understand that this type of self-examination holds us accountable to ourselves as well as to the Inner Witness. There really is not a set of expected answers, only an expectation that God will engage me through the contemplation of the question, encouraging me to accept the truth that I discover. As we practice the art of thanking and blessing, this contemplative engagement helps us discover the blessing of acting with integrity—that is to say, with consistency between values and actions.

For instance, if your reflection on priorities led to the conclusion that peace was important to you, then it would be appropriate to investigate how you tend or promote this priority. Start with a look at inner peace. Are you at ease with yourself and your lot in life, or do you discover layers of anger and conflict seething beneath the surface? Do your own self-care and spiritual practice address the issues that disrupt your state of inner peace?

From that point, you could consider your manner of engaging others with whom you have differences or disagreements. Do you possess and practice adequate skills of negotiation and conflict resolution so that peaceful outcomes are achieved?

If these skills serve you well in your interpersonal relationships, you could consider being a peacemaker in your community. Through your involvement with community affairs, can you model careful listening and respectful response as a means of wrestling with difficult issues?

When you turn your attention to a global perspective and discover that much violence and conflict result from greed or scarcity, and that the United States consumes far more of the world's resources than its population merits, a commitment to peace might challenge you to reduce consumption or shop differently. It will make virtually no dent in the flow of supply and demand, but it is an important statement about the alignment of values and conduct.

It is an easy thing to say that we value peace, or that we desire peace. Living in a manner that demonstrates a commitment to that value requires a bit of contemplation, decision, and, in all probability, change. We all know that change can be uncomfortable, even painful. However, we experience a real joy and gratitude from knowing that we are living "within our own skin"—that the conduct of our lives supports those things that matter most deeply to us.

Another story from Quaker lore illustrates this type of integrity in action, even when costly. Historian Max Carter tells of a man named Matthew Osborne, an eighteenth-century Quaker from Centre Friends Meeting in North Carolina. Osborne was a "Jamestown Rifle" gunsmith who manufactured and sold guns to several people in the surrounding area for the purposes of hunting. As war with England loomed, many Quakers remained neutral on the proposed revolution, as the avoidance of war was an important testimony of their faith.

When the Revolutionary War began, Osborne was severely troubled by the thought that guns made by his hands might be used in war to kill other human beings. According to the report, he went to each of his customers and purchased his rifles from all who would sell them. He then heated the gun barrels and bent them so that they could not fire a shot. That was a costly move, but his strong convictions about war made this a move of integrity.

Talk is cheap; the call for integrity stems from a desire that the actions of our lives speak louder than our words. As we travel the path of thanking and blessing, we discover our true self, reclassified in light of the new insights we have garnered from this faith perspective. To fully benefit from the potential blessing this discovery introduces, we will need to embody the insights and perspectives it reveals. In many instances, decisions of integrity will no doubt challenge us, but they will, without exception, enrich the quality of life for those fortunate enough to be affected by us. Even as love, hospitality, and hope frame our interactions, we will also need to demonstrate that we are reliable and trustworthy. We accomplish this through actions that testify to the gratitude that grounds us, and we demonstrate our commitment to the values and perspectives we espouse.

At times, this comes at a price, as not everyone always appreciates that you are working from a place of integrity. While on vacation in New Orleans several years ago, Judi and I relented to the requests of a person who accosted us on the street to listen to a timeshare presentation. We were not interested in the purchase and said as much. The salesperson was confident we would change our minds. We ultimately decided the free tickets being offered in exchange for our time were a fair trade, and we agreed to participate.

The person assigned to us followed up on my self-identification as a Quaker. What did it mean? Among other things, I said it meant that our word was our bond. If I were not interested in his product, I would say so. If I were interested, my first offer would be my best and only offer.

As we listened to the presentation, we actually began to think about the possibility of buying not one, but two weeks at the resort. If we owned the weeks during Mardi Gras and the Sugar Bowl, we reasoned, we could easily rent them and the place would pay for itself. We asked detailed questions. We listened to the sales pitch. Much to our surprise, we made an offer, lower than their asking price, but one that we thought was fair. You probably can guess the next step. The salesperson needed to consult with her manager. Fifteen minutes later she returned, disgusted with her supervisor. He could not take our offer, but he had sent a counterproposal. We smiled, thanked her for her time, and rose to leave. A look of confusion masked her face. Where were we going? Was there no counteroffer? We reminded her of the discussion we had had at the outset regarding what a Quaker was. Our first offer was our best offer, and our only offer. Upon being reminded of that, she prepared to go back to her supervisor a second time. She felt sure he would accept our offer if he knew we were about to leave. We refused to allow them a second chance, asking what kind of statement it made about their approach to business if our first offer was a fair price, but they had chosen to try and gouge us unfairly. We preferred, whenever possible, to reserve our business for people we could trust to deal fairly with us. I think this is the only time I have been shouted at when exiting a business.

Our words are important, but integrity is about more than words. It includes a basic commitment to represent ourselves fairly and accurately. It involves keeping our commitments to one another—doing what we say we will do, arriving when we say we will arrive, leaving when we say we will leave. It includes acts of basic decency, such as taking responsibility for our own actions, even if those actions did not go as well as others expected.

It means fulfilling the commitments we make to others, if for no other reason than we gave them our word.

Integrity is ultimately about living lives that support our words, and it may even speak louder than words as we embrace the priorities we identify for ourselves.

EXPERIMENTING WITH INTEGRITY

Your life has many facets to it. You have personal desires, family responsibilities, and professional and social obligations. You may feel that others place heavy demands and expectations on you. How do you navigate these many expectations in a way that ensures that your responses mirror your deepest values? If you want to have a life of integrity, you will need to compare your desires with the current order of your life.

1. To begin, make a simple list of the things you believe are your top priorities. You may discover your list includes personal goals you wish to achieve or qualities you want to exhibit. Perhaps it will include spiritual practices you wish to integrate into your daily life, or your hopes for change in the world. As long as you believe it is a top priority for yourself, it belongs on the list.

2. When your list is complete, analyze how you invest your resources of self, time, and energy.

   • Does the way you speak reflect the priorities of the list?
   • Does the way you spend your time support any of your priorities?
   • Do your actions match your priorities?

It is not unusual for people to discover that they are not spending their time or resources in pursuit or support of the things they say they value. If that is the case for you, consider ways to align the lists. Reorder how you commit your time and energy. Alternatively, consider the possibility that you really hold a different set of values and priorities than you thought. This is the necessary mental and spiritual work you need to do to gain the clarity required for living with integrity. As you gain that clarity, let it manifest itself in everyday routines.

- Let your word be your bond, simple and true, as the New Testament quotation that opened this chapter reminds us. As easy as that may sound, it will in many cases seem like you alone are operating by a different set of rules—even as you let your yes be yes, you will find that many are not so forthright.
- If a tranquil life is a priority, commit to cultivating that peaceful state of being.

  - Eat slowly, savoring each bite.
  - When traveling, leave a few minutes early so that you won't have to rush.
  - Before answering someone, measure your response to ensure it conveys your thoughts in truthful but loving ways.

- If spending more quality time with family is a priority that needs attention, make a commitment to do so.

  - Decide what you will sacrifice in order to be available to your family.
  - Make a concerted effort to leave work on time.
  - Give up one extracurricular activity that you do without your family and spend that time with them. Identify activities the entire group finds meaningful and spend time together enjoying those things.

- If you discover a desire to be more involved in your community, look for opportunities where your strengths can be utilized.
  - What do you have to offer that would be an asset to the community?
  - Are there volunteer organizations where your energy could make a difference?

In any of these, or in other scenarios, construct your involvement and interaction in ways that are consistent with the practices outlined in chapters 1 through 8. It is of little value to espouse the riches of thanking and blessing if the practices are not in evidence in your own circles of influence.

The identification and subsequent alignment of values and commitments create a harmonious integrity of body, mind, and spirit. You will spend your time on the things that you value, and you will value the ways that you spend your time. If that is the case, the fatigue that settles over you at the end of a long day will be seasoned with joy, satisfaction, and a sense of unity with God. You will feel gratitude for this life that is meaningful. Being committed to a spirituality of thanking and blessing, the likelihood is great that those commitments, whatever they are, will be carried out in a spirit of love and hospitality that blesses those who meet you along the way.

CHAPTER TEN

TASTE AND SEE

My wife, Judi, loves to share food with me. Whether it is a new recipe she prepares in our kitchen or a five-star dessert at a favorite restaurant, sharing the experience with me is as important to her as tasting it herself. Her commitment to sharing reminds me of a similar devotion to spiritual sharing displayed in the psalmist's words: "Taste and see how good the Lord is" (Ps. 34:9). The psalmist is so moved by his experience of God that he can't help but want to share it.

We reach a comparable place in the sacred art of thanking and blessing. The spiritual practices we learn along this path create a feast of communion with the Divine and the delightful world in which we live. In time, we want others to understand the benefits of this practice for themselves. Like the psalmist, we will want to invite others to taste and see these rich and pleasurable experiences.

But how do we share? Communication, especially about spiritual things, can be a tricky business. When it comes to describing profound experiences, sometimes words get in the way. I remember standing at the edge of the Grand Canyon, feeling overwhelmed, small, and insignificant. If you have ever been there, you know the feeling, and you also know words could never convey the experience—not the colors, not the shadows, not the echoes. You can read up on all the guidebooks and talk to others who've been there, yet nothing really prepares you for the moment you first step to the edge of that canyon rim. For me, it was overwhelming, dwarfing—practically a holy moment. Maybe it *was* a holy moment.

I have been fortunate enough to travel widely, and have had similar experiences at the Luxor Temple in Egypt, Machu Picchu in Peru, and the Vietnam Memorial in Washington, D.C. These were moments when I was barely able to comprehend beauty or achievement or ingenuity or tragedy, moments when I felt entirely merged with the Oneness of life that unites us all. I can never find the words to adequately describe it. Photos don't help much either! Standing on holy ground, the clearest communication I could muster was to point in its direction.

The moment we begin to reduce such experiences to words and images, we objectify them. We move from living in the present moment to talking about it instead. Spiritual practice as a topic discussed is not the same as a spirituality *experienced*. It is difficult to convey adequately the lasting impact the art of thanking and blessing has upon our perception of God and the world around us.

Yet, we can at least take others to the edge of the canyon, as it were, and point toward the source of our own wonder and amazement. Words may not do justice to the spiritual wonder we want to describe, but if we can lead others to the threshold, standing there on the edge, they can have their own powerful, life-changing experience. They have the opportunity to say "yes" to God's invitation to try something mysterious, frightening, important, and even holy—"to taste and see that the Lord is good."

THE DESIRE AND RESPONSIBILITY TO SHARE

As we grow in our care for the world and for others, we want to bring people to the edge of the canyon where they can experience this blessed reality for themselves, for two explicit reasons. One of the reasons we want to share the practice of thanking and blessing that we have discovered is simply so others can be edified. Remember, blessing desires good for others! What has proved to be enriching and life-changing for us may have a similar, positive effect on others. Without thought of personal gain or ulterior motives, we gladly introduce others to these experiences as well. We want them to feel the same wonder of gratitude that wells up within us. We desire to share the beauty and promise of life lived in awareness of divine blessing.

But we also yearn to share our practice because the art of thanking and blessing is an effective antidote to much of the world's suffering and pain. Violence, prejudice, poverty, greed— these are all realities in our world, yet they are aberrations of the intentions for goodness and blessing knit into the fabric of creation. What are we to do in the face of this solemn reality? The sacred art of thanking and blessing counters those frightened perspectives with a universe of love and compassion.

Even so, the scale of this world's problems can feel overwhelming. To be honest, some days I would like to ignore the world's suffering and pain and retreat into my own safe, little world. That is not a good option, but the alternative is hard work. I was complaining to a friend recently about the difficulty of working against these systemic problems. Maybe it was better just to give up, I suggested. He laughed, and reminded me that once we are aware of a given issue, we have a responsibility to do what we can to help overcome it.

If my friend is right, then silence in the face of the world's suffering is not an option. We have an obligation to give voice to the new insights that have grasped our attention. We have a responsibility to encourage others to draw up to the canyon's edge. This is a task that we can easily want to shirk, because it gives our words a prophetic edge—that is to say, our words may call for transformation and may not be popular with everyone who hears them.

The prophet Jeremiah of the Hebrew Bible lamented the message he felt God compelled him to give. He described his impulse like this: "I thought, 'I will not mention Him, no more will I speak in His name'—but His word was like a raging fire in my heart, shut up in my bones; I could not hold it in, I was helpless" (Jer. 20:9). Hopefully, we will be spared Jeremiah's lament, but not his internal conviction. When Jesus taught about the distinctiveness that religious conviction adds to a person's perspective, he described believers as the light of the world that could help illumine the paths for others when they shared their light (Matt. 5:14–16). His teaching implied that those who have light have a responsibility to shine.

Even this is not a mandate from outside ourselves, but rather something that arises organically from our own practice. As we cultivate the art of thanking and blessing, we glimpse the Oneness of life. Just as we cannot suppress our joy, neither can we repress our outrage at the suffering, nor escape a growing sense of responsibility to speak out against it. We find ourselves lodged between two difficulties: the difficulty of describing the power of those transformative experiences of the Divine, and the difficulty of remaining silent when we feel compelled to address the more troubling issues that surround us. Thankfully, the hope that arises in this sacred art dreams of a better world, and it provides stamina and fortitude for the cause. For all of these reasons—the joy of sharing, the heartache we witness, and the hope for success—we will want to find appropriate ways to share and communicate the power we have come to know. We will be unable to resist the desire to contribute positive energy to the cycle of life around us because we understand the deep connection we all share. We now sense the possibilities and responsibilities that lay before us as we awaken to the reality of the divine blessing that accompanies us.

THE ART OF SHARING WELL

Equally important is the matter of how we choose to express ourselves, because whether we are encouraging and nurturing others, or objecting to actions and attitudes out of harmony with thanking and blessing, effective communication is an art. It becomes even more delicate given the balance we seek to achieve between love and integrity. It becomes even trickier when our sharing takes on the potential prophetic edge.

Whatever message we want to deliver, it is best filtered through the priorities of love, hospitality, and integrity, no matter how positive or how difficult the message may be. Our heartfelt objective is to invite and encourage all to taste and see the wonder of the Divine so that gratitude and blessing begin to permeate their lives.

One of the unique challenges we face when speaking about spiritual things is that people don't always hear what we say, or at least what we mean. When I served as a pastoral minister, one of the most fascinating snippets of weekly conversation was during those moments greeting people as they exited the building after worship. Their description of what they heard me say and the meaning they inferred from my words was often quite different than what I had intended. I was originally disturbed by this, and I wondered how I could communicate more clearly. But over time, I came to enjoy that disconnect between my words and what the congregation heard as a mystery of God's movement. Congregation members were working to find meaning for their lives. At the intersection of my words, their experience, and the movement of God, they were finding meaning that surpassed anything I could offer.

We may also face resistance as we try to share our perspective. This often has to do with the fact that throughout history, and still today, many religiously motivated people have been known to choose the route of domination and oppression as they inflict their light upon others. This is one reason so many of us are reluctant to engage the spiritual quest or to affiliate with religious groups. This unfortunate reality is a direct result of the issue addressed in chapter 1—where we start the story has a powerful effect on its development and conclusion. When the faith story begins with humanity being depraved and in need of rescue, unfortunately, often self-appointed rescuers end up subjugating others to their paradigm of truth.

Domination has no place in the practice of thanking and blessing. Instead, we are free to come alongside others like a companion on the journey. From that vantage point, our lives can speak regarding the value and integrity of the path of thanking and blessing. We can offer hospitality—in effect, be a blessing to those we have come alongside. As we walk with them, we can walk supportively in their difficult moments and bless them with love and kindness as opportunities present themselves.

A third challenge has to do with the pluralistic context of our modern world. Pluralism has helped us learn tolerance, but it has generally not taught us how to live respectfully or engage people of other faiths with love and integrity. As practitioners of thanking and blessing, we cannot long abide that misstep, because we possess, or are possessed by, a prophetic quality. We aim to get along and learn from one another, it's true; we are also actively contributing to people's lives, offering them pronouncements of hope and divine favor and goodwill. This style of communication finds expression in multiple traditions:

> The spirit of the Lord God is upon me, because the Lord has anointed me; He has sent me as a herald of joy to the humble, to bind up the wounded of heart, to proclaim release to the captives, liberation to the imprisoned; to proclaim a year of the Lord's favor and a day of

vindication by our God; to comfort all who mourn …
(Isa. 61:1–2)

One should speak the truth and speak it pleasingly;
should not speak the truth in an unpleasant manner nor
should one speak untruth because it is pleasant; this is the
eternal law. (*Laws of Manu* 4.138)[1]

If you are aware of a certain truth, if you possess a jewel,
of which others are deprived, share it with them in a language of utmost kindliness and goodwill. If it be
accepted, if it fulfills its purpose, your object is attained. If
anyone should refuse it, leave him unto himself and
beseech God to guide him. Beware lest you deal unkindly
with him. (*Epistle to the Son of the Wolf*, 15)[2]

The art of thanking and blessing promotes a positive and uplifting spirituality, but it should not be confused with an idealistic
viewpoint that lives in denial of the great rifts that exist in the
human family. Our differences are many: race, religion, ethnicity, class, and culture, to name a few. These differences are not
themselves the rifts, but they often perpetuate practices and
opinions that create chasms of separation. In the face of this
potential discord I have found the words of Jesus to be particularly helpful: "Be wise as serpents but as innocent as doves"
(Matt. 10:16). This is sound advice as we consider how to help
perpetuate blessing in the universe, especially in those areas
dominated by ignorance and injustice. Travelers on this spiritual
path accept that there are moments when they must speak, and
that they must do so in the right tone and spirit.

NOT AN AGENDA

If balancing all these concerns seems daunting, it's helpful to
remember a couple of things. First, we are all part of One, and

therefore the person to whom you speak has a deep and important connection to you. You may not like a particular person much, for any number of reasons. The good news is, there is that of God in her, just as there is that of God in you. When you speak to her, your Inner Witness is dialoguing with her Inner Witness. Her Inner Sanctuary can open the way to transforming encounters with the Divine, just as it has done with you.

A friend of mine shared a useful phrase with me recently. Early in our friendship it was obvious that she enjoyed working in tense, even conflicted, situations, often with people who manifested unappealing behaviors. That day we were discussing an opportunity she had to work as a chaplain in a women's prison. It would provide opportunities for occasional preaching, offering pastoral care, providing spiritual direction, and working with peace and justice issues affecting the inmates. When I asked how attention to her own interior spirituality had prepared her for this work, she gave a wonderful reply: "Now that I have my internal house organized, I am not afraid to accompany those who are suffering."

That is the spirit in which practitioners of thanking and blessing address the world. We can manifest gratitude and blessing in all settings, with anyone, because divine love and blessing have "organized our house" and prepared us to engage the universe as friend, and even as part of ourselves. We know no fear, even in the face of heartache, because we have discovered the inner strength of blessing. Based on what we know of God, of blessing, of love, we realize that we have something to say—a message of hope—and that we can say it well.

Second, our sharing is motivated by love, not by an agenda. Ordinarily, prophets intend to be persuasive—they attempt to affect change by winning or converting people to their point of view. It is precisely here that the spirituality of thanking and blessing diverges from the traditional path of the prophet.

Instead of goading others to a decision we want them to make, we make space for others to make up their own mind. We come to know experientially that this is God's world, not ours. We do not control the Divine, and we do not own the world. We are made in God's image, but that does not mean that we are to remake the world according to our preferences. Ours is a spirituality of invitation, not domination. Admittedly, this is a difficult strategy because decisions against the practice of thanking and blessing slow the creativity of the Spirit at work among us. Nonetheless, integrity of purpose and respect for others requires this of us.

You will no doubt note that this chapter has stopped well short of defining what your message will be in these situations. It is not my place to form the content of your message. I can describe the spiritual context, the desired dialogue with the Creator, the defining characteristics of a spirituality of thanking and blessing. When it comes to the message, however, the standing question in old Quaker language is "What can'st thou say?" With the established relationship and ongoing dialogue you sustain with the Divine, as you live in the image of God, what is your message? What can you say in the face of joy? What will you offer to the hungry or heartbroken? Part of the great joy of thankful living and lives of blessing is that we recognize the grand invitation to become creative agents in the ongoing work of God. One way we do that is through the creative power of words and the prophetic dance that weaves them into the flow of life's activities so that their meaning breaks open, illuminating life's greatest mysteries and possibilities.

EXPERIMENTING WITH SHARING

For the generous of spirit, sharing comes easily. The extroverts among us will always find a way to express their thoughts and feelings. For the rest of us, sharing takes conscious effort and lots of practice. The gratitude that grows within us as we practice this sacred art helps push us into the thick of life, where we have the opportunity to make a positive difference in the world. With time, the care we develop for all of creation instills a desire to share acts of blessing to the degree we are able to do so. The Oneness we discover teaches us of the cyclical nature of thanking and blessing—what goes around, comes around. When we love and bless others, we love and bless ourselves, too. As this awareness emerges within us, we face the practical task of learning how to share in ways that promote the spirituality of thanking and blessing.

- You cannot really share until you know what you have to offer. This means you need to engage in conscious reflection about your spiritual encounters.

  - When you experienced the Divine in the quiet of expectant waiting, what did you feel? Did you hear or see anything? What thoughts ran through your mind?
  - Did the experience move you?
  - Can you discern any wisdom, insight, or truth from those moments? How will you describe that insight?

At the school where I am dean, we spend a lot of time working with students on these types of questions. Our goal is to help them discover their own theological and spiritual vocabulary so that they can talk about their experience of God and begin to give voice to their spiritual journey.

- As a first step toward sharing the richness of your spiritual journey, develop your vocabulary. Keep a small notebook in your pocket and when fresh images or language describing your experience of God comes to mind, write it down so that you remember it.

- Begin to use that emerging vocabulary to describe your faith perspective with an integrity that rings true to your experience.

As you develop a spiritual vocabulary, you deepen your own understanding of how the Divine is moving in your life. As that understanding grows, begin to ask questions about relevance.

- So what if you believe that God is love? How does that influence the way you see the world? Would it change the way you live as one made in the image of God?
- Where love is absent, or at least not obvious, do you have a responsibility to help take others to the edge of the canyon so that they might experience the wonder?
- If love ran rampant in the world, what would change?

The last question invites you to speculate. Leaps of faith require speculation, where you consider the multiple possibilities of what could be if certain conditions were met. If you want to experiment with sharing gratitude and blessing in ways that demonstrate the prophetic edge Jeremiah had, you will need to develop an opinion on lots of topics.

- As a result of your conversations with God and care for others, what convictions do you hold on topics such as:
  - Racism
  - Domestic violence
  - Living wages
  - Deficit spending
  - Employers allowing maternity and paternity leave
  - The introduction of casinos in your city
  - Western imperialism

Thoughtful opinions are the conclusions you reach as you speculate on the various possibilities in light of your understanding of the relevant facts and feelings associated with a matter. Opinion solidifies your engagement with the world—which you can carry out in a spirit of gratitude and blessing dedicated to working for the common good based on your experience of the Divine.

To make this task of sharing more manageable, consider the following question.

- If you were called to be an ambassador of thanking and blessing at this moment, what one message would you share? In seven words or less, create a means to express it.
- Consider making those seven words your prayer refrain, mantra, or chorus for the day. Let it accompany you throughout the day. Expect it to gently shape your conversations and actions. Look for ways to interject it into conversations, and invite others to respond to what you have offered.

In a similar, contemplative mode, consider what forces and structures disrupt or deny the peace and tranquility in your life.

- Ask the same question with regard to the forces that interfere with the occurrence of blessing in your community.
- As things come to mind, be sure to examine your motives and objectives.
- When you sit in expectant waiting with these things on your heart, to what does the Inner Witness call you? In Quaker terms, this is the discovery of "what can'st thou say?" Such speaking can be tense at times, because the message will likely challenge others, even when spoken in gentle tones.

- Identify what you need in order to deliver the message in the spirit of gratitude and blessing.
- Take your message to the community.
  - Write an op-ed piece or editorial for the local newspaper.
  - Convene a neighborhood interest group to share your concerns and ideas for addressing them. If your message resonates with others in the group, you may have just served as a catalyst for change.
  - If you own a business, analyze the ethos and practices of your business to make sure it embodies the ideals associated with the art of thanking and blessing—this is not a closet or Sunday-only spirituality. If the message cannot thrive in the marketplace, you are still missing part of the big picture.
- Finally, take inventory of the inner calm that increases as you live as a creative agent for the sake of thanking and blessing.

Life may be busy, but it can be rich and rewarding. The journey that began as a discovery of who you are created to be has come full circle, now celebrating your new and emerging role as a co-creator. It is good. You are blessed. Indeed, you yourself are a blessing.

NOTES

INTRODUCTION
1. See especially John 1, 3, 8, 9, 11, and 12 for use of the term *light*.

CHAPTER 1
1. *The Laws of Manu: Sacred Books of the East,* vol. 25, trans. George Bühler, in Internet Sacred Text Archive, http://www.sacred-texts.com/hin/manu/manu01.htm (accessed February 1, 2007).
2. *The Medicine Rite Foundation Myth, Version 5,* trans. Oliver LaMére, in Norton William Jipson, *Story of the Winnebagos* (Chicago: The Chicago Historical Society, 1923), 409–11, at http://www.hotcakencyclopedia.com/ho .CreationOfWorld.html (accessed May 13, 2007).
3. Abraham J. Heschel, *Moral Grandeur and Spiritual Audacity: Essays.* (New York: Farrar, Straus and Giroux, 1997), 264.

CHAPTER 2
1. Thomas Kelly, *A Testament of Devotion* (San Francisco: Harper and Brothers, 1941), 9–10.
2. John Punshon, *Encounter with Silence* (London: Quaker Home Service, 1987), 60.
3. Robert Barclay, *Barclay's Apology*, in the Digital Quaker Collection, http://dqc.esr.earlham.edu (accessed February 5, 2007), 357.
4. Isaac Penington, "Way of Life and Death Made Manifest," in *Works of the long-mournful and sorely-distressed Isaac Penington,* vol. 1, ed. Isaac Penington, George Fox and William Penn, in

the Digital Quaker Collection, http://dqc.esr.earlham.edu (accessed February 21, 2007), xlvi.

CHAPTER 3

1. *Karaniya Metta Sutta*, trans. D. J. Gogerly, in "Four Short Suttas" *Journal Asiatique* 20 (1872): 226-31, in Internet Sacred Text Archive, http://www.sacred-texts.com/journals/ ja/tbg.htm (accessed February 22, 2007).

CHAPTER 4

1. George Fox, *The Journal of George Fox,* ed. Rufus M. Jones (1908; repr., Richmond, VA: Friends United Press, 1976), 82.
2. Peace Pilgrim, "Steps Toward Inner Peace," http://www.peacepilgrim.com/steps1.htm (accessed January 7, 2007).
3. *Karaniya Metta Sutta.*
4. William Penn, "Primitive Christianity Revived," in *Collection of the Works of William Penn*, vol. 2, in the Digital Quaker Collection, http://dqc.esr.earlham.edu (accessed February 5, 2007), 858.

CHAPTER 6

1. David O'Neal, *Meister Eckhart from Whom God Hid Nothing* (Boston: Shambhala Publications, 1996), 6.
2. His Holiness the Dalai Lama, *The Path to Tranquility: Daily Wisdom,* ed. Renuka Singh (1998; repr., New York: Penguin Compass, 2002), 329.
3. Samuel Macpherson Janney, *History of the Religious Society of Friends,* vol. 2, in the Digital Quaker Collection, http://dqc.esr.earlham.edu (accessed February 1, 2007), 206.
4. *Karaniya Metta Sutta.*

CHAPTER 7

1. "ghosti," in *The American Heritage Dictionary of the English Language,* 4th ed. (Boston: Houghton Mifflin, 2000), www.bartleby.com/61/ (accessed January 13, 2007).
2. *Taittiriya Upanishad*, trans. Swami Gambhirananda, I.XI.2, www.geocities.com/advaitavedant/taittiriya.htm (accessed January 15, 2007).

CHAPTER 8

1. Penington, 134.

CHAPTER 9

1. Samuel M. Janney, *The Life of William Penn; with Selections from His Correspondence and Auto-Biography* (Philadelphia: Hogan, Perkins, and Co., 1852), 42–43.

2. *Quaker Faith & Practice: Third Edition*, http://quakersfp.live .poptech.coop/qfp/chap1/1.02.html (accessed February 22, 2007).

CHAPTER 10

1. *The Laws of Manu: Sacred Books of the East.*

2. *Epistle to the Son of the Wolf*, in the Baha'i Academic Resource Library, http://bahai-library.org/writings/bahaullah/esw/ default.html (accessed January 5, 2007), 15.

SUGGESTIONS FOR FURTHER READING

Baha'i Academic Resource Library. http://bahai-library.org/writings/bahaullah/esw/default.html/.

Barclay, Robert. *Barclay's Apology*. Philadelphia: Benjamin Stanton, 1831. http://dqc.esr.earlham.edu.

Bill, J. Brent. *Mind the Light*. Brewster, MA: Paraclete Press, 2006.

Birkel, Michael. *Silence and Witness*. Maryknoll, NY: Orbis, 2004.

Bokser, Ben Zion, trans. *The Talmud Selected Writings*. New York: Paulist Press, 1989.

Bühler, George, trans. *The Laws of Manu: Sacred Books of the East*, vol. 25. Oxford: Oxford University Press, 1886. http://www.sacred-texts.com/hin/manu/manu01.htm.

Eck, Diana L. *Darsan: Seeing the Divine Image in India*, 2nd ed. Chambersburg, PA: Anima Books, 1985.

Ford, Marcia. *Finding Hope: Cultivating God's Gift of a Hopeful Spirit*. Woodstock, VT: SkyLight Paths Publishing, 2007.

———. *The Sacred Art of Forgiveness: Forgiving Ourselves and Others through God's Grace*. Woodstock, VT: SkyLight Paths Publishing, 2006.

Fox, George. *The Journal of George Fox*. Edited by Rufas M. Jones. 1908. Reprint, Richmond, IN: Friends United Yearly Meeting, 1976.

Fox, Matthew. *Original Blessing*. Santa Fe, NM: Bear & Company, 1983.

Frymer-Kensky, Tikva, David Novak, Peter Ochs, et al. *Christianity in Jewish Terms*. Boulder, CO: Westview Press, 2002.

Gambhirananda, Swami. *Taittiriya Upanishad*. Kolkatta: Advaita Ashram. http://www.geocities.com/advaitavedant/taittiriya.htm.

Gogerly, D. J. trans. *Karaniya Metta Sutta,* in "Four Short Suttas" *Journal Asiatique* 20 (1872): 226-31, in Internet Sacred Text Archive, http://www.sacred-texts.com/journals/ja/tbg.htm.

His Holiness the Dalai Lama. *The Path to Tranquility: Daily Wisdom.* Edited by Renuka Singh. 1998. Reprint, New York: Penguin Compass, 2002.

Janney, Samuel M. *The Life of William Penn; with Selections from His Correspondence and Auto-Biography.* Philadelphia: Hogan, Perkins, and Co., 1852.

————. *History of the Religious Society of Friends.* 4 volumes. Philadelphia: Hayes and Zell, 1860. http://dqc.esr.earlham.edu.

Kelly, Thomas. *A Testament of Devotion.* San Francisco: Harper and Brothers, 1941.

The Koran. University of Michigan Digital Library. http://www.hti.umich.edu/k/koran/.

Lamére, Oliver, trans. *The Medicine Rite Foundation Myth, Version 5.* In Norton William Jipson, *Story of the Winnebagos* (Chicago: The Chicago Historical Society, 1923). http://www.hotcakencyclopedia.com/ho.CreationOfWorld.html.

O'Neal, David. *Meister Eckhart from Whom God Hid Nothing.* Boston: Shambhala Publications, 1996.

Penington, Isaac, George Fox, William Penn, eds., *Works of the long-mournful and sorely-distressed Isaac Penington.* 3rd ed. London: J. Phillips, 1784. http://dqc.esr.earlham.edu.

Penn, William. *A Collection of the Works of William Penn*, vol. 2. London: J. Sowle, 1726. http://dqc.esr.earlham.edu.

Prager, Marcia. *The Path of Blessing: Experiencing the Energy and Abundance of the Divine.* Woodstock, VT: Jewish Lights Publishing, 2003.

Punshon, John. *Encounter with Silence.* London: Quaker Home Service, 1987.

Quaker Faith & Practice: Third Edition. http://quakersfp.live.poptech.coop/qfp/.

Sawyer, Nanette. *Hospitality—The Sacred Art: Discovering the Hidden Spiritual Power of Invitation and Welcome.* Woodstock, VT: SkyLight Paths Publishing, 2007.

Shapiro, Rami. *The Sacred Art of Lovingkindness: Preparing to Practice.* Woodstock, VT: SkyLight Paths Publishing, 2006.

"Steps Toward Inner Peace." http://www.peacepilgrim.com/steps1.htm/.

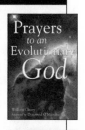

Spirituality & Crafts

The Knitting Way: A Guide to Spiritual Self-Discovery
by Linda Skolnik and Janice MacDaniels
7 x 9, 240 pp, Quality PB, b/w photographs, 978-1-59473-079-5 **$16.99**

The Quilting Path: A Guide to Spiritual Discovery through Fabric, Thread and Kabbalah
by Louise Silk
7 x 9, 192 pp, Quality PB, b/w photographs and illustrations, 978-1-59473-206-5 **$16.99**

The Scrapbooking Journey: A Hands-On Guide to Spiritual Discovery
by Cory Richardson-Lauve; Foreword by Stacy Julian
7 x 9, 176 pp, Quality PB, 8-page full-color insert, plus b/w photographs
978-1-59473-216-4 **$18.99**

Spiritual Practice

Divining the Body: Reclaim the Holiness of Your Physical Self
by Jan Phillips
A practical and inspiring guidebook for connecting the body and soul in spiritual practice. Leads you into a milieu of reverence, mystery and delight, helping you discover your body as a pathway to the Divine.
8 x 8, 256 pp, Quality PB, 978-1-59473-080-1 **$16.99**

Finding Time for the Timeless: Spirituality in the Workweek
by John McQuiston II
Simple, refreshing stories that provide you with examples of how you can refocus and enrich your daily life using prayer or meditation, ritual and other forms of spiritual practice. 5½ x 6¾, 208 pp, HC, 978-1-59473-035-1 **$17.99**

The Gospel of Thomas: A Guidebook for Spiritual Practice
by Ron Miller; Translations by Stevan Davies
An innovative guide to bring a new spiritual classic into daily life.
6 x 9, 160 pp, Quality PB, 978-1-59473-047-4 **$14.99**

Earth, Water, Fire, and Air: Essential Ways of Connecting to Spirit
by Cait Johnson 6 x 9, 224 pp, HC, 978-1-893361-65-2 **$19.95**

Labyrinths from the Outside In: Walking to Spiritual Insight—A Beginner's Guide
by Donna Schaper and Carole Ann Camp
6 x 9, 208 pp, b/w illus. and photos, Quality PB, 978-1-893361-18-8 **$16.95**

Practicing the Sacred Art of Listening: A Guide to Enrich Your Relationships and Kindle Your Spiritual Life—The Listening Center Workshop
by Kay Lindahl 8 x 8, 176 pp, Quality PB, 978-1-893361-85-0 **$16.95**

Releasing the Creative Spirit: Unleash the Creativity in Your Life
by Dan Wakefield 7 x 10, 256 pp, Quality PB, 978-1-893361-36-2 **$16.95**

The Sacred Art of Bowing: Preparing to Practice
by Andi Young 5½ x 8½, 128 pp, b/w illus., Quality PB, 978-1-893361-82-9 **$14.95**

The Sacred Art of Chant: Preparing to Practice
by Ana Hernández 5½ x 8½, 192 pp, Quality PB, 978-1-59473-036-8 **$15.99**

The Sacred Art of Fasting: Preparing to Practice
by Thomas Ryan, CSP 5½ x 8½, 192 pp, Quality PB, 978-1-59473-078-8 **$15.99**

The Sacred Art of Forgiveness: Forgiving Ourselves and Others through God's Grace
by Marcia Ford 8 x 8, 176 pp, Quality PB, 978-1-59473-175-4 **$16.99**

The Sacred Art of Listening: Forty Reflections for Cultivating a Spiritual Practice
by Kay Lindahl; Illustrations by Amy Schnapper
8 x 8, 160 pp, b/w illus., Quality PB, 978-1-893361-44-7 **$16.99**

The Sacred Art of Lovingkindness: Preparing to Practice
by Rabbi Rami Shapiro; Foreword by Marcia Ford
5½ x 8½, 176 pp, Quality PB, 978-1-59473-151-8 **$16.99**

Sacred Speech: A Practical Guide for Keeping Spirit in Your Speech
by Rev. Donna Schaper 6 x 9, 176 pp, Quality PB, 978-1-59473-068-9 **$15.99**
HC, 978-1-893361-74-4 **$21.95**

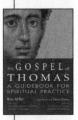

Spirituality of the Seasons

Autumn: A Spiritual Biography of the Season
Edited by Gary Schmidt and Susan M. Felch; Illustrations by Mary Azarian
Rejoice in autumn as a time of preparation and reflection. Includes Wendell Berry, David James Duncan, Robert Frost, A. Bartlett Giamatti, E. B. White, P. D. James, Julian of Norwich, Garret Keizer, Tracy Kidder, Anne Lamott, May Sarton.
6 x 9, 320 pp, 5 b/w illus., Quality PB, 978-1-59473-118-1 **$18.99**
HC, 978-1-59473-005-4 **$22.99**

Spring: A Spiritual Biography of the Season
Edited by Gary Schmidt and Susan M. Felch; Illustrations by Mary Azarian
Explore the gentle unfurling of spring and reflect on how nature celebrates rebirth and renewal. Includes Jane Kenyon, Lucy Larcom, Harry Thurston, Nathaniel Hawthorne, Noel Perrin, Annie Dillard, Martha Ballard, Barbara Kingsolver, Dorothy Wordsworth, Donald Hall, David Brill, Lionel Basney, Isak Dinesen, Paul Laurence Dunbar. 6 x 9, 352 pp, 6 b/w illus., HC, 978-1-59473-114-3 **$21.99**

Summer: A Spiritual Biography of the Season
Edited by Gary Schmidt and Susan M. Felch; Illustrations by Barry Moser
"A sumptuous banquet.... These selections lift up an exquisite wholeness found within an everyday sophistication."— ★ *Publishers Weekly* starred review
Includes Anne Lamott, Luci Shaw, Ray Bradbury, Richard Selzer, Thomas Lynch, Walt Whitman, Carl Sandburg, Sherman Alexie, Madeleine L'Engle, Jamaica Kincaid.
6 x 9, 304 pp, 5 b/w illus., Quality PB, 978-1-59473-183-9 **$18.99**
HC, 978-1-59473-083-2 **$21.99**

Winter: A Spiritual Biography of the Season
Edited by Gary Schmidt and Susan M. Felch; Illustrations by Barry Moser
"This outstanding anthology features top-flight nature and spirituality writers on the fierce, inexorable season of winter.... Remarkably lively and warm, despite the icy subject." — ★ *Publishers Weekly* starred review
Includes Will Campbell, Rachel Carson, Annie Dillard, Donald Hall, Ron Hansen, Jane Kenyon, Jamaica Kincaid, Barry Lopez, Kathleen Norris, John Updike, E. B. White.
6 x 9, 288 pp, 6 b/w illus., Deluxe PB w/flaps, 978-1-893361-92-8 **$18.95**
HC, 978-1-893361-53-9 **$21.95**

Spirituality / Animal Companions

Blessing the Animals: Prayers and Ceremonies to Celebrate God's Creatures, Wild and Tame *Edited by Lynn L. Caruso* 5 x 7¼, 256 pp, HC, 978-1-59473-145-7 **$19.99**

What Animals Can Teach Us about Spirituality: Inspiring Lessons from Wild and Tame Creatures *by Diana L. Guerrero* 6 x 9, 176 pp, Quality PB, 978-1-893361-84-3 **$16.95**

Spirituality

Awakening the Spirit, Inspiring the Soul
30 Stories of Interspiritual Discovery in the Community of Faiths
Edited by Brother Wayne Teasdale and Martha Howard, MD; Foreword by Joan Borysenko, PhD
Thirty original spiritual mini-autobiographies showcase the varied ways that people come to faith—and what that means—in today's multi-religious world.
6 x 9, 224 pp, HC, 978-1-59473-039-0 **$21.99**

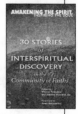

The Alphabet of Paradise: An A–Z of Spirituality for Everyday Life
by Howard Cooper 5 x 7¼, 224 pp, Quality PB, 978-1-893361-80-5 **$16.95**

Creating a Spiritual Retirement: A Guide to the Unseen Possibilities in Our Lives
by Molly Srode 6 x 9, 208 pp, b/w photos, Quality PB, 978-1-59473-050-4 **$14.99**
HC, 978-1-893361-75-1 **$19.95**

Finding Hope: Cultivating God's Gift of a Hopeful Spirit
by Marcia Ford 8 x 8, 200 pp, Quality PB, 978-1-59473-211-9 **$16.99**

The Geography of Faith: Underground Conversations on Religious, Political and Social Change *by Daniel Berrigan and Robert Coles* 6 x 9, 224 pp, Quality PB, 978-1-893361-40-9 **$16.95**

God Within: Our Spiritual Future—As Told by Today's New Adults *Edited by Jon M. Sweeney and the Editors at SkyLight Paths* 6 x 9, 176 pp, Quality PB, 978-1-893361-15-7 **$14.95**

About SKYLIGHT PATHS Publishing

SkyLight Paths Publishing is creating a place where people of different spiritual traditions come together for challenge and inspiration, a place where we can help each other understand the mystery that lies at the heart of our existence.

Through spirituality, our religious beliefs are increasingly becoming a part of our lives—rather than *apart* from our lives. While many of us may be more interested than ever in spiritual growth, we may be less firmly planted in traditional religion. Yet, we do want to deepen our relationship to the sacred, to learn from our own as well as from other faith traditions, and to practice in new ways.

SkyLight Paths sees both believers and seekers as a community that increasingly transcends traditional boundaries of religion and denomination—people wanting to learn from each other, *walking together, finding the way.*

For your information and convenience, at the back of this book we have provided a list of other SkyLight Paths books you might find interesting and useful. They cover the following subjects:

Buddhism / Zen	Gnosticism	Mysticism
Catholicism	Hinduism /	Poetry
Children's Books	Vedanta	Prayer
Christianity	Inspiration	Religious Etiquette
Comparative	Islam / Sufism	Retirement
Religion	Judaism / Kabbalah /	Spiritual Biography
Current Events	Enneagram	Spiritual Direction
Earth-Based	Meditation	Spirituality
Spirituality	Midrash Fiction	Women's Interest
Global Spiritual	Monasticism	Worship
Perspectives		

Or phone, fax, mail or e-mail to: SKYLIGHT PATHS Publishing
Sunset Farm Offices, Route 4 • P.O. Box 237 • Woodstock, Vermont 05091
Tel: (802) 457-4000 • Fax: (802) 457-4004 • www.skylightpaths.com
Credit card orders: (800) 962-4544 (8:30AM–5:30PM ET Monday–Friday)
Generous discounts on quantity orders. SATISFACTION GUARANTEED. Prices subject to change.

For more information about each book,
visit our website at www.skylightpaths.com